A Concise History
of
Rock 'n' Roll

KEVIN W. BUCK

Year of the Book
135 Glen Avenue
Glen Rock, PA 17327

Print ISBN: 978-1-949150-12-4
eBook ISBN: 978-1-949150-13-1

Library of Congress Control Number: 2018951793

FOR GALE

Thank you for tolerating my jumps from Sinatra to Metallica and everything in between (sometimes in the same playlist!). Your love and support helped me get this over the finish line.

ACKNOWLEDGMENTS

Over the course of developing this book, I received a lot of feedback/thoughts from friends and reviewers. My short list of people I particularly want to acknowledge include Gale Buck, Imre Vitez, Tom Volpe, Ruth Anna Abigail, Barbara Yutzy, and Concetta Bagnato for their invaluable help.

I also want to acknowledge Demi Stevens of Year of the Book Press for bringing her Swiss Army knife of publishing skills to the table as well as her breadth of musical knowledge. She is a true gem.

CONTENTS

FOREWORD

R ock 'n' Roll[1] is the first music type to span generations. Music that youth enjoyed in the '20s was ignored in the '30s. Music from the '30s was ignored in the '40s and so on – that is until Rock 'n' Roll hit the mainstream in the '60s.

Every generation wants a variant of popular music they can call their own. The difference with Rock 'n' Roll is that new generations embrace previous variants as well as the new.

While attending a concert recently, Led Zeppelin's "Black Dog" was being played, at a very high volume, in between bands. I looked around and saw teenagers, young teenagers at that, singing along with Robert Plant and emulating Jimmy

---

[1] I have chosen to use the term "Rock 'n' Roll" versus "Rock and Roll," "Rock & Roll," or other variations. I feel that this use captures the spirit of the music.

Page's riffs on air guitar. This occurred despite their parents probably not yet being born when the song was released. That drove home to me that Rock 'n' Roll is here to stay. It's going to change, but it will thrive.

Talking with many people (older as well as younger), I found a general ignorance of Rock 'n' Roll history, other than some of the legends/myths, such as Ozzy Osbourne biting the head off a bat. Looking at what books were available to bring people up to speed, I found spotty material that only covered a narrow view. This is what drove me to write this book.

Why am I qualified to write the book? Good question. I'm glad you asked. I am a late baby boomer and the youngest of five, which exposed me to many different types of music starting with the '60s. My brother Bob introduced me to '60's Folk and The Ventures. Brother Ken gave me The Doors and Frank Zappa. Sister Sandy was a diehard Beach Boys fan. John, my childhood friend, and I would discuss and debate the Allman Brothers, Grand Funk, and so much more.

I have always enjoyed music, but what took that interest to the next level was when my brother, Gary, offered to let me go with him to concerts starting in the early '70s. My first concerts included Foghat, KISS, Queen, and many other bands considered rock royalty today. That sunk the hook deep, and music – especially live music – will be a part of me forever.

One of the harder parts of writing this book was differentiating between Rock 'n' Roll versus Pop music. Since Pop is short for Popular, Rock can be considered Pop if it reaches mainstream airplay. The lines drawn are 100% mine and may not match up with yours, but I am hoping that you, the reader, will cut me a little slack.

I am writing this book for the person who wants a good base understand of Rock 'n' Roll's history. I will also provide "homework assignments" for those wanting to dig deeper.

Look for this symbol for additional learning paths:

I hope you enjoy the book and that it sparks an interest and maybe even sinks the hook for you, as it did for me. I know that I will leave out some items others deem important. For that, I apologize in advance, but also encourage you to contact me with your thoughts/corrections. Let's do this!

ROOTS

R ock 'n' Roll comes out of the merging of many different music types. A lot of people align themselves with a single music type and I will never understand why. Good music is good music, no matter what genre it came from or when it was recorded. Why limit yourself to a small section of the salad bar when a full buffet is available? Don't make blanket statements like "I don't like country or rap." I'm sure there are some songs in every genre that will float your boat. Keep an open mind and treat new music like I treat wine: I don't know anything about it, but I can tell you whether I like it or not after giving it a fair trial.

I am going to cover, at a high-level, the core music genres that shaped Rock 'n' Roll into what we have today. I'm sure rock historians around the world will condemn me for my simplistic approach, but my goal is to make this consumable for a general audience and offer paths for those who want to learn more.

Blues

"The origins of blues is not unlike the origins of life. For many years it was recorded only by memory, and relayed only live, and in person. The Blues were born in the North Mississippi Delta following the Civil War. Influenced by African roots, field hollers, ballads, church music and rhythmic dance tunes called jump-ups evolved into a music for a singer who would engage in call-and-response with his guitar. He would sing a line, and the guitar would answer. The Blues... its 12-bar, bent-note melody is the anthem of a race, bonding itself together with cries of shared self-victimization. Bad luck and trouble are always present in the Blues, and always the result of others, pressing upon unfortunate and down trodden poor souls, yearning to be free from life's troubles. Relentless rhythms repeat the chants of sorrow, and the pity of a lost soul many times over. This is the Blues.[2]"

This quote captures the essence and roots of the Blues. While I will cover other contributing genres below, Blues is the true cornerstone of Rock, and every serious student of music should feel compelled to study it further. This music, which originates out of pain, sadness, boredom, and sorrow, tells a personal story that strikes emotional chords at a visceral level. Those Rock songs with power chords that make most men strike their air guitar pose can be tied back to songs being played at Mississippi Delta juke joints in the 1920s.

---

[2] www.history-of-rock.com

It is important to understand that the core Blues musicians of yesteryear were a major influence on Rock stars past, present, and future. Robert Johnson's subtle voice inflections, Lead Belly's songs about current events, Muddy Waters' electrified update to the Blues, and so many other musicians inspired the likes of Chuck Berry, The Beatles, Eric Clapton, Keith Richards, and Jimi Hendrix.

Huddie Ledbetter
(Lead Belly)

Robert Johnson's "Terraplane Blues"

Books:	***Blues Fell This Morning: Meaning in the Blues*** Paul Oliver (Cambridge University Press, 1990)
	Deep Blues: A Musical and Cultural History of the Mississippi Delta Robert Palmer (Penguin Books, 1982)
Video:	***The Blues*** (Vulcan Productions/PBS, 2003)
Road Trip:	***Delta Blues Museum*** 1 Blues Alley, Clarksdale, MS 38614
	National Blues Museum 615 Washington Ave, St. Louis, MO 63101

Rhythm and Blues

Rhythm and Blues (R&B) rose from the ashes of the Big Band era where a new music style was needed that brought the energy of the Big Bands and Swing, but could be made with a smaller group of musicians. A steady beat, with the mix of Jazz and Blues influences, which was tagged as Rhythm and Blues, emerged from the late 1940s into the mid-1950s. The dominant star of the late '40s was Louis Jordan who had 18 Number 1 singles on the R&B charts and 54 singles in the Top Ten.

Record companies only marketed R&B music to urban African-Americans, but in the early to mid-'50s, white teenagers took notice and started buying more and more R&B records. "Little" Richard Penniman started recording as an R&B artist, but by the mid-'50s had evolved his funky, up-tempo R&B skills to come up with what most people refer to as the first generation of Rock 'n' Roll. R&B would continue to evolve over the years to incorporate elements of Gospel, Doo Wop, Soul, Pop, Hip-hop and many other music variants.

Louis Jordan

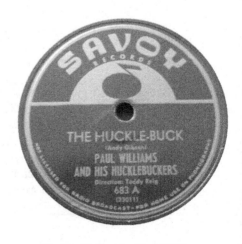

The Huckle-Buck by Paul Williams

Books:	***Rhythm and the Blues: A Life in American Music*** (Wexler/Ritz Knopf, 2012)
Video:	***Rhythm and Blues at the Apollo Theatre*** (Storyville Films, 2004)
Road Trip:	***Memphis Rock and Soul Museum*** 191 Beale Street, Memphis, TN 38103

Country

Country music's roots can be traced back to Celtic ballads brought to America by British immigrants. By the early 1920s, what started off as mountain music had incorporated vocal harmonies and become more popular across the U.S. with the advent of records and radio. Jimmie Rodgers is generally considered the father of recorded Country music and is credited with the first million-selling single, "Blue Yodel #1," released in 1928.

In 1925, the Grand Ole Opry radio show began as a one-hour "barn dance" program. The show was expanded to four hours in the '30s and became a Saturday night tradition in almost 30 states. The singing cowboys in the movies of the '30s and '40s—such as Gene Autry and Roy Rogers—further broadened its appeal. Variations of Country music, generally by region, started to emerge. Honky Tonk was an overnight sensation in the late '40s, making stars of Ernest Tubb and Hank Williams. Tonk is one of the few Country styles that refuses to evolve and its fans rejoice.

Jimmie Rodgers

Hank Williams

Books:	**Country Music, U.S.A.** Malone/Neal (University of Texas Press, 3rd Ed., 2010)
Listen to:	**Blue Yodel #1** Jimmie Rodgers (Camden, NJ, 1927)
	I Walk the Line Johnny Cash (Sun, 1956)
	I'm So Lonesome I Could Cry Hank Williams (MGM, 1949)
	Crazy Patsy Cline (Decca, 1962)
	Mama Tried Merle Haggard (Capitol, 1968)
Road Trip:	**Country Music Hall of Fame** 222 5th Ave S, Nashville, TN 37203

PLAYBACK

In order to fully understand the historical context of Rock, you also need to understand how the delivery mechanisms evolved along with the music. For time eternal, musicians have played live music for groups in large venues, such as concert halls, and in small venues, such as dance halls, clubs, and people's front parlors. The introduction of Thomas Edison's Phonograph cylinders in 1877 started the consumer sound revolution with the ability to record and playback sounds with pre-recorded cylinders being introduced in 1889. The device included a large horn to amplify the sound. The downside of the cylinder was that it was a cardboard tube covered in wax and would wear down each time it was played, eventually becoming unusable.

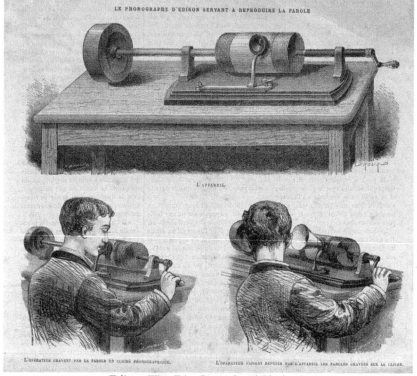

Edison Wax Disc Record and Playback

In the 1890s, flat disc records[3] made of shellac (a brittle material) were introduced, making cylinders obsolete due to being more durable and easily reproduced. The industry standardized on these discs rotating at 78 Rotations Per Minute (RPM) with the 10-inch version of the 78 RPM record holding about three minutes of music. Longer songs had to be split across multiple records[4]. Commercial radio stations

---

[3] Short for "recording."
[4] These records were stored in paper sleeves that were bound together on one edge like a book. Now you know where the term "album" comes from!

blossomed in the 1920s with 60% of U.S. households having a radio by 1930. The stations played music, but they also broadcast news, soap operas, comedians, etc. Dedicated music channels were a rarity. The rise of Popular music is generally attributed to the radio with Big Band stars such as Benny Goodman, and singers like Bing Crosby.

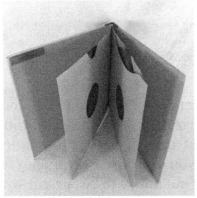

An "Album"   Old Time Radio

78 RPM records lasted until after World War II when they were replaced by 12-inch vinyl records being played at 33 1/3 RPM, allowing about 20 minutes of sound on each side. (These longer playing records were commonly referred to as "LPs.") Smaller vinyl records spinning at 45 RPM that contained a single song on each side (a.k.a. "singles" and "45s") quickly followed. Transistor technology enabled the creation of smaller radios in the 1950s and allowed listeners to unplug from the wall to listen virtually anywhere. This especially benefited the youth who no longer had to rely on family-shared devices to listen to their music.

Transistor Radio   Diner Table Jukebox   Full Size Jukebox

Coin-operated music boxes have been around almost as long as recorded music, but from the early 1940s to the mid-1960s, jukeboxes became an important part of American culture, particularly for young people. If you didn't have the money for your own record player or could not afford to be current with the latest singles, you could drop a coin into the jukebox at the local diner and select the song of your choice. The art of jukeboxes, such as bright colors, flashing lights, and bubbles, make them a cultural touchstone for many generations.

Most commercial radio use was based on AM[5] technology, despite FM[6] technology being around since the 1930s and providing superior sound quality. In the early 1960s, the Top 40 radio programming model was born. By surveying the top-played songs on jukeboxes and via radio station request calls, the Top 40 songs began to be played in a heavy rotation.

In 1964, the first mainstream use of magnetic tape debuted via the 8-track tape which could hold approximately 45 minutes of music. While there were other magnetic tape formats available, the widespread use of 8-track tape devices in

---

[5] "Amplitude Modulated" where the signal strength is varied to incorporate sound.
[6] "Frequency Modulated" where the frequency (the number of times each second that the current changes direction) is varied to incorporate sound.

automobiles made it a runaway success[7]   until cassettes became available in the early '70s.

Most AM radio stations re-broadcast their signal on their FM station, but were forced to stop due to a FCC non-duplication rule in 1967. The languishing FM stations needed to be used quickly, so many allowed the use of free-form Rock 'n' Roll formats. This occurred right in the middle of the counter-culture movement of the '60s and was the perfect platform for music that did not fit the AM mold. Playing longer/non-Top 40 songs, complete album sides and anything else they felt like playing earned FM the reputation of being an "underground" entity making their listeners the avant-garde.

In 1979, Sony introduced the Walkman cassette player. Portable radios had been available since the mid-'50s, but now you had a personalized, high quality audio experience on the go and the concept of a "mix tape" was born. You could create tapes to match a given theme or a particular mood and was quickly adopted by runners and commuters everywhere. By 1983, cassettes outsold vinyl for the first time, primarily due to the Walkman, with exciting new features like auto-reverse and two earphone jacks.

8-Track Tape   Cassette Tape   Compact Disc

---

[7] The downside of 8-tracks was that if a piece of music was longer than the tape, you had to endure a sharp "clack" noise as the device jumped between tracks.

In 1983, the Compact Disc (CD) was released. Finally we had a playback technology that did not wear down with each playback[8]. There are still audiophiles who prefer the sound reproduction of vinyl, but what I miss most is the artwork and liner notes that went into a vinyl album cover. By the mid-'90s, we could store audio files, such as MP3s, on our computers and in today's world we have the ability to stream virtually any music, any time, to almost any device using the internet.

For each of these playback types, you need to put yourself into the context of the time. Imagine that it's 1969 and you had read in a Rock magazine[9] that your favorite group was going to release a new album. You would check in with your record store on a regular basis until you finally got the release date and then had to patiently wait. When the date finally arrived, you went to the store, bought the record, and took it home. You took the shrink wrap off, read whatever notes there were on the cover, took the album out of the paper sleeve and finally put it on your turntable. You carefully eased the needle down onto the outer rim of the record and sat back to finally listen. Once side one was completed, you flipped it over and listened to side two. If you had some like-minded friends you might even have a listening party.

Rituals are an important part of any music fan's life. I can still remember the thrill of hearing a new Beatles album, the first Jimi Hendrix album, and the KISS *Alive!* album. It's not that music fans today don't look forward to their band's upcoming releases, but due to our immediate gratification times, the ritual and all of its elements seem lost.

---

[8] Vinyl wore out and magnetic tape stretched and broke down over time. I think it was part of the record company's business model to count on replacing worn out media.
[9] Rock magazines like *Circus* and *Rock Scene* were printed months in advance and it was difficult to stay current with what was going on in the music business.

According to a recent survey by MusicWatch[10], almost half of vinyl record purchasers are under 25. I am encouraged by the resurgence of vinyl as a playback medium, and in particular, by a generation where most of their parents never witnessed a needle drop onto vinyl. This group now gets to relive the rituals of the past and all its associated joys.

---

[10] http://www.musicwatchinc.com/research-studies/music-acquisition/

EARLY ROCK 'N' ROLL PHASES

Rock 'n' Roll has morphed and changed so much over the years, it would be easy to get mired down in the details of each tangent, but that is not the goal of this book. Please note that all categorization is mine and that bands, and our perception of them, evolve over time.

Pink Floyd was both a "Progressive" as well as "Psychedelic" band. When the Talking Heads and Blondie first came out, they were considered "Punk" (primarily due to them being regular performers at CBGBs in New York City), but were later defined as "New Wave." Today most people would put them in either the Pop or Classic Rock category.

I present to you, from the perspective of a late baby-boomer (and the chagrin of many music historians), the major phases of Rock 'n' Roll. I realize that to paint the history of Rock 'n' Roll in such broad strokes will upset a few, but my hope is that it will educate more than I anger. I will do my very best to do justice to each phase.

Early Rock

The song that most historians point to as the first major milestone in rock is 1955's[11] "Rock Around the Clock" by Bill Haley and His Comets, which was the first Rock 'n' Roll song to hit the top of the Pop charts, but so much happened leading up to that milestone.

The emergence of Rock 'n' Roll in the '50s and early '60s was during the post-World War II period when America was in one of its most prosperous phases ever. There was a mass exodus to the suburbs with teenagers' tastes and buying power starting to drive what was produced. Up to this point, record stores, radio stations, and other media outlets marketed Blues, Rhythm and Blues, and Jazz music solely to African-Americans. When white teenagers started to buy this music in large volumes, the record companies took notice and expanded their catalog to satisfy the demand. This opened the door for Rock 'n' Roll pioneers like Chuck Berry, Little Richard, Bo Diddley, and many more. This was not an overnight occurrence. We had to get past the "cover" phase where white artists, like Pat Boone and Perry Como, covered songs initially released by black artists.

---

[11] 1955 is a flash point in Rock 'n' Roll history with the release of Bill Haley's "Rock Around the Clock," Bo Diddley's "I'm a Man," Little Richard's "Tutti Frutti," and Chuck Berry's "Maybellene."

Bill Haley & His Comets   The Five Satins

Doo Wop

Doo Wop is based on Rhythm and Blues, but relies heavily on vocal harmonization. Its origins can be traced back to earlier vocal groups like the Ink Spots. One of the first big Doo Wop hits was 1954's "Sh-Boom" by The Chords. Its success opened the door for The Platters, The Coasters, The Five Satins, and many more.

Doo Wop was very successful on the Pop charts in the mid-to-late '50s, and by 1961, had reached its zenith with The Marcels' "Blue Moon."

Books:	*Making Your Memories with Rock & Roll and Doo-Wop: The Music and Artists of the 1950s and Early 1960s* (iUniverse, 2016)
Video:	*Life Could Be a Dream - The Doo Wop Sound* (Bayview Entertainment, 2003)
Listen to:	*Blue Moon* The Marcels (Colpix, 1961)
	Earth Angel The Penguins (Dootone, 1954)
	Sixteen Candles The Crests (Coed, 1958)
	Why Do Fools Fall In Love Frankie Lymon & The Teenagers (Gee, 1956)
	In the Still of the Night The Five Satins (Standord, Ember, 1956)
Road Trip:	*The Doo Wop Preservation League Museum* 4500 Ocean Avenue, Wildwood, NJ 08260

Teen Idols

Paul Anka, Fabian, Bobby Rydell, Frankie Avalon, Gene Pitney, and Ricky Nelson sent teenage girls into frenzies in the 1950s and early 1960s. Music teen idols were not a new thing. Rudy Vallée, Frank Sinatra, and many others had been idolized before, but with the advent of television, it seemed idols were being made, and cast aside for the next, at a breakneck pace. It was definitely a formula, but, hey, as long as the music is good...

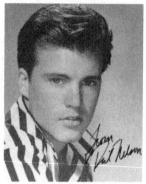

| Fabian with Ed Sullivan | Frankie Avalon | Ricky Nelson |

Books:	*Bobby Rydell: Teen Idol On The Rocks: A Tale of Second Chances* (Doctor Licks Publishing, 2016)
Video:	*Rock N Roll's Greatest Teen Idols* (MVD Entertainment, 1999)
Listen to:	*Wild One* Bobby Rydell (Cameo, 1960)
	Dream Lover Bobbie Darin (Atco, 1959)
	Travelin Man Ricky Nelson (Imperial Records, 1961)
	Diana Paul Anka (ABC, 1957)
	The Night has a Thousand Eyes Bobby Vee (Liberty, 1962)

Rockabilly

"We shook the devil loose! We bopped those blues! It's uptempo, it's rhythm. You ain't sitting there worrying about car payments or house notes. You're out there shakin dust loose on those honky-tonk floors."[12]

Carl Perkins defined the '50's Rockabilly[13] style with 1956's "Blue Suede Shoes." It was a bold, unafraid mix of R&B and Country that generally included just a twangy lead guitar, a stand-up bass, and the drums. Occasionally a piano would be included, but it serves as the most stripped-down, basic variant of Rock. The vocals included lots of yips, yelps, gulps, and echo effects. Elvis Presley's early recordings, such as "That's Alright Mama," are the best know Rockabilly songs.

Sun Records in Memphis, Tennessee, seemed to be a lightning rod for Rockabilly talent with Elvis, Johnny Cash, Roy Orbinson, Carl Perkins, and Jerry Lee Lewis among the talent whose careers were launched at Sun. Rockabilly seems to go through a revival cycle every few years. The most recent successes were The Stray Cats and Brian Setzer's solo career.

Left to right: Carl Perkins, Roy Orbison, Johnny Cash, and Jerry Lee Lewis

---

[12] Carl Perkins, as noted on page 16 of Bill Flanagan's book, *Written in My Soul* (Contemporary Books, 1986).
[13] The Rockabilly name is a blend of "rock" and "hillbilly," reflecting the blending of Rock 'n' Roll with Country music.

Books:	*The Rockabilly Legends: They Called It Rockabilly Long Before They Called It Rock and Roll* (Hal Leonard Corporation, 2007)
Video:	*It's a Rockabilly World* (Virgil Films and Entertainment, 2016)
Listen to:	*Blue Suede Shoes* Carl Perkins (Sun, 1956)
	That's Alright Mama Elvis Presley (Sun, 1954)
	Summertime Blues Eddie Cochran (Liberty, 1958)

The Pioneers

Elvis Presley – There is a full chapter on Elvis later in the book, but I have included him here to recognize the fast company he was running in. Many people who heard his songs on the radio were sure that he was black, and there are some who claim Elvis stole black music, but I don't have the qualifications to discuss that. What I do know is that Elvis had a lot of talent and he was the right person, in the right place at the right time to cement Rock 'n' Roll as a color-blind American phenomenon.

Bo Diddley – Bo was a cutting edge singer, songwriter, producer, and inventor (check out his square guitar). The "Bo Diddley Beat" used in his song of the same name, and many others, is still prominent among artists today.

Bill Haley & His Comets – The importance of the song "Rock Around the Clock" cannot be overstated. While the band did not look too cool dressed in matching, plaid dinner jackets, and Bill's spit curl was distracting, their song serves as the first, significant landmark in Rock 'n' Roll history.

Chuck Berry – Chuck was the premier Rock 'n' Roll lead guitar player. His songs and many TV appearances established the sound and the attitude of Rock we know today. His music inspired The Beatles, The Rolling Stones and countless others. Taking him out of the Rock 'n' Roll equation would give us a different, and I'm sure less satisfying, result.

Little Richard – Combining superb musicianship and a flamboyant performing style, Little Richard crushed the racial barrier to bring Rock 'n' Roll to the masses. The National Recording Registry of the Library of Congress stated that his "unique vocalizing over the irresistible beat announced a new era in music."

Jerry Lee Lewis – Lewis' fire-breathing, burn-down-the-house piano playing genuinely scared parents, but the youth were captivated by his electric performances. The scandal of marrying his first cousin's 13-year-old daughter slowed down his career, but Jerry never lost the fire. Elvis said that if he could play the piano like Lewis he would quit singing.

Fats Domino – Fats did not think of his playing as Rock 'n' Roll, but rather the New Orleans version of Rhythm and Blues. In any case, his influence and smooth piano playing over a Pop/Rock beat caught our attention and we never let go.

Buddy Holly – Buddy accomplished a lot in his short career. He wrote, recorded, and produced all of his own music and is considered the artist who defined the standard Rock 'n' Roll line-up of lead guitar, rhythm guitar, bass guitar, and drums. His death at age 22, along with Richie Valens and J. P. Richardson Jr. (known as "The Big Bopper"), is the basis for Don McLean's song "American Pie."

Chubby Checker – Chubby has many amazing accomplishments, including being the only artist to have five albums in the Top 12. In my opinion, his biggest accomplishment was getting adults out on the dance floor with his song, "The Twist." Prior to that, adults just did not dance to teenagers' music, and in doing this, he broadened the acceptance of Rock 'n' Roll.

Elvis Presley

Bo Diddley

Chuck Berry

Buddy Holly

Video:	*Let the Good times Roll* (Columbia, 1973)
Listen to:	*That's Alright Mama* Elvis Presley (Sun, 1954)
	I'm a Man Bo Diddley (Checker 814, 1955)
	Ain't That a Shame Fats Domino (Imperial, 1955)
	That'll Be The Day The Crickets[14] (Brunswick, 1957)
	Great Balls of Fire Jerry Lee Lewis (Sun, 1957)

---

[14] While the band would later be referred to as Buddy Holly and the Crickets, Buddy had recorded the song in 1956 as Buddy Holly and the Three Tunes, but the contract prohibited him from re-recording the song for five years. Crediting The Crickets was a way around this.

THE FATHER OF
ROCK 'N' ROLL

The term "rock and roll" was used for hundreds of years to refer to the rocking and rolling of an ocean voyage. By the early 20th century, it became slang for a style of dancing/partying as well as sex. The first recorded song to use the term was 1922's "My Man Rocks Me (with one steady roll)" by Trixie Smith. The term "Rock 'n' Roll", as we use it today, was coined by Cleveland disc jockey Alan Freed in 1951 to describe the mix of Rhythm, Blues, and Country music he was playing on his radio show.

Alan Freed

Alan Freed went on to be part of many other milestones in Rock 'n' Roll history:

- He produced the first Rock concert: "The Moondog Coronation Ball" held on March 21, 1952, at the Cleveland Arena. It did not get beyond the first act's first song due to the overselling/counterfeiting of tickets. The fire authorities shut things down when 20,000 people showed up at the 10,000-seat venue. Freed's early concerts cast the mold for the modern Rock concert.

- He starred in the first Rock 'n' Roll movies:

  o *Rock Around the Clock*, Columbia Pictures, 1956
  o *Rock, Rock, Rock*, Vanguard Productions, 1956
  o *Mister Rock and Roll*, Paramount Pictures, 1957
  o *Don't Knock the Rock*, Columbia Pictures, 1956
  o *Go, Johnny, Go!* Valiant Films, 1959

- He hosted the shortest, successful Rock 'n' Roll TV show. In 1957, Alan was given a primetime show on ABC called "The Big Beat." Despite good ratings, the show was cancelled after four weeks. In one of the episodes,

Frankie Lymon, a black singer, was seen dancing with a white girl from the audience. The complaints to the ABC affiliates in the South resulted in the show's cancellation.

- He was part of the first Rock 'n' Roll scandal: It was referred to as "payola": the practice of accepting money to promote specific records. The legality of this practice was very controversial and led to Freed being fired. He was then charged with "commercial bribery," for which he paid a fine and received a suspended sentence.

- He was the first DJ charged with inciting a riot: In Boston, Freed was charged with "inciting the unlawful destruction of property" under the Massachusetts anti-Anarchy Law. The police claimed that when they refused to let Freed lower the house lights for the performance at a May 3, 1958 show, he said, "It looks like the Boston police don't want you to have a good time." Other eyewitness reports claim it was Jerry Lee Lewis who said it, but in any case, the incident led to bans on Rock 'n' Roll concerts around the country.

- He is a member of the first group inducted into the Rock 'n' Roll Hall of Fame.

- He is the first (and only) person to have his remains in the Rock 'n' Roll Hall of Fame. The urn with Freed's ashes was on display from 2002 to 2014. His remains are now interred at Cleveland's Lake View Cemetery.

Video:	*The Alan Freed Story - The Early Years Of Rock & Roll* (Collectables Press, 2007)
Listen to:	*My Man Rocks Me (with one steady roll)* Trixie Smith, from *The Complete Recorded Works, vol 2* (1925-1939) (Document Records, 2000)

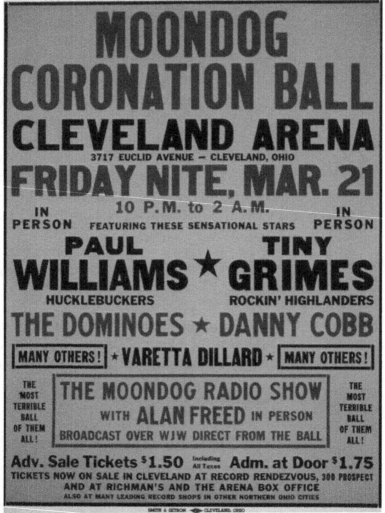

The first rock concert was a failure in that 20,000 people could not fit into a space designed for 10,000, but it did demonstrate that there was an audience for rhythm & blues and the emerging hybrid, Rock 'n' Roll.

60's ROCK

T he 1960's Rock 'n' Roll universe went through many drastic changes. It started as a continuation of the late '50's style with the crooning of pompadour-clad teen idols such as Bobby Rydell and Ricky Nelson. Elvis was out of the army and about to start his film career, Chubby Checker's

Twist songs created an international dance craze, but some major changes were brewing.

Folk Music

Folk music goes back for centuries, but I will focus on what is referred to as "contemporary" folk music. The roots of contemporary Folk started with Woody Guthrie during the Depression of the 1930s. Folk had a following in the '40s and '50s, but the stripped down, storytelling style lent itself to the verbalization of the political, lifestyle, and counterculture changes occurring during the '60s. The Vietnam War and civil rights movement were two strong themes in '60's Folk music and its influence inevitably splashed into the Rock 'n' Roll world.

The breakout Folk artists of the '60s were:

- Joan Baez – Dubbed the "Barefoot Madonna" for her otherworldly voice, Joan first performed at the 1959 Newport Folk Festival and her first three albums stayed on the Billboard charts[15] for over two years. She was one of the first major artists to record Bob Dylan songs and after almost 60 years of performing and 30 albums, Joan was inducted into the Rock 'n' Roll Hall of Fame in 2017.

- Kingston Trio – While known primarily for their version of the song "Tom Dooley," the Kingston Trio was responsible for the mainstreaming of the Folk music style. Fourteen of their 19 albums were in the Billboard Top 10 with five hitting the number one spot.

- Bob Dylan – Bob Dylan's first album did not sell well and Columbia Records wanted to dump his contract. Thank goodness they gave him another shot. The list of classic

---

[15] The Billboard charts were a weekly composite of single sales, album sales, and radio airplay used to measure the success of a song or album. They now include various digital distribution channels such as streaming.

songs he released in the early '60s is long: "Blowin' in the Wind"[16], "A Hard Rain's a-Gonna Fall," "The Times They Are a-Changin'," "It Ain't Me Babe," and many more. Bob had appeared, with great success, at the 1963 and 1964 Newport Folk Festival. In 1965, he decided to play electric guitar at the festival and was booed off the stage after playing only three songs[17].

- Peter, Paul and Mary – They came together at the time when the first wave of baby-boomers were entering college and developing a social conscience. Their songs, such as "Lemon Tree," "If I had a Hammer," "Puff the Magic Dragon," and many Bob Dylan covers, hit the balance of making young people think about their place on the earth and commercial success.

Joan Baez and Bob Dylan

---

[16] Based on the melody from the traditional slave song "No More Auction Block."
[17] There are some claims that the boos were due to Dylan's short set, but all the coverage went to the outraged Folk community who felt betrayed by Bob Dylan plugging in.

Books:	***Folk City: New York and the American Folk Music Revival*** (Oxford University Press, 2015)
Video:	***Legends of Folk: The Village Scene*** (PBS, 2011)
Listen to:	***The Lily Of The West*** Joan Baez (Vanguard, 1961)
	Blowin' In The Wind Bob Dylan (Columbia, 1962)
	Puff (the Magic Dragon) Peter, Paul and Mary (Warner Music Group, 1963)

The Beatles

The influence of The Beatles on Rock music cannot be understated, which I will address in a separate chapter, but I wanted to call them out here so as to give you a context for what was going on during their emergence.

A lot of young people I talk to don't care for The Beatles' music and while I always respect their musical opinion, I want them to respect what The Beatles did for Rock 'n' Roll. Their music was probably the biggest influence on music, of any genre ever, and will continue to be so for a long time.

Surf Rock

Dick Dale kick-started the Surf Rock genre as pure instrumentals with guitars using heavy reverb[18] and a fast tempo. His signature song is a cover of "Misirlou" (an Eastern Mediterranean folk song) and is considered the baseline for all surf instrumentals.

A second generation started with The Beach Boys and Jan & Dean layering pop harmonies over the traditional Surf Rock

---

[18] The reverb setting on Fender amps of the era, when maxed out, produced a tone that evoked images of crashing surf. Dedicated reverberation devices became standard fare in 1960's recording studios.

beat with some historians considering it an extension of Doo Wop.

The Surf music wave crested in 1963, but fell off with the British Invasion in 1964. The Beach Boys, who eventually resented being categorized as a "Surf Rock" band, had the only long term, mainstream success and even fed the Psychedelic Rock phase.

It's interesting to note that The Beach Boys and The Beatles motivated each other in a reciprocal manner. When Brian Wilson, primary songwriter for the Beach Boys, first heard The Beatles' "Rubber Soul," he lamented, "They got there first!" and cried. The next day Brian wrote "God Only Knows" and was so inspired by The Beatles new album, he decided not to tour with his group, and instead settled in to write his masterpiece album *Pet Sounds*. That album, in turn, was part of the inspiration for The Beatles to write *Sgt. Pepper's Lonely Hearts Club Band,* which in turn motivated The Beach Boys' album *Smile.* Musicians are always going to influence each other and if these two great music legends did so, imagine the thousands of other musicians influenced by these bands.

The Beach Boys on *The Ed Sullivan Show*

Books:	***Surf Beat: Rock 'n' Roll's Forgotten Revolution*** Kent Crowley (Hal Leonard Corporation, 2011)
Video:	***Endless Harmony: The Beach Boys Story*** (Capitol Records/EMI, 2000)
Listen to:	***Misirlou*** Dick Dale (Del-Tone, 1962)
	Surfin' USA The Beach Boys (Capitol, 1963)
	Dead Man's Curve Jan and Dean (Liberty, 1962)
	Wipe Out The Safaris, DFS, Princess (Dot, 1963)

Garage Rock

With influences from many areas of music including Surf Rock and the British Invasion, Garage Rock focused on a simplistic approach to making music with little regard to sound quality and an anti-establishment attitude. The "garage" moniker comes from the perception of an amateurish band practicing, and maybe even recording, in the family garage. While this was rarely the case, it was the spirit and enthusiasm of the music that grabbed the listener and held on. Common themes around the generally raw sound were lyrics describing the trials of high school life and lying girlfriends. Most Rock historians look to Garage Rock as the precursor to the '70's Punk Rock.

The Kingsmen

The Standells

Books:	*Garage Rock and Its Roots: Musical Rebels and the Drive for Individuality* Eric James Abbey (McFarland & Company, 2006)
Listen to:	*Louie, Louie* The Kingsmen (Jerden 712, 1963)
	Hang on Sloopy The McCoys, (Bang 506, 1965)
	96 Tears Question Mark and the Mysterians and Rudy Martinez (Pa-Go-Go/Cameo-Parkway, 1966)
	Dirty Water The Standells (Tower, 1965)

British Invasion

With the breakout of The Beatles in 1964, the floodgates opened for other British bands into America. Earlier attempts to copy U.S. formulas failed, but the Jazz-influenced Skiffle[19] craze encouraged a "do it yourself" model that drew out the talents of musician wanna-bes everywhere. This flood included The Kinks, The Rolling Stones, The Dave Clark Five, Dusty Springfield, Herman's Hermits, The Animals, The Yardbirds, Wayne Fontana and the Mindbenders, Peter and Gordon, and many, many more.

The Animals   The Kinks

---

[19] Skiffle is a Jazz-inspired music style that actually started in the U.S. that relied on improvised instruments such as washboards, cigar box fiddles, washtub bass, and paper kazoos. It had faded out of the U.S., but was revived in England in the mid-1950s by Lonnie Donegan. John Lennon and several other future invaders cut their teeth in Skiffle bands.

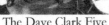
The Dave Clark Five

The Rolling Stones

By May of 1965, British bands had nine of the top 10 songs[20]. This deluge of bands did several things:

- It internationalized Rock music and U.S. fans would no longer be content with just homegrown bands.
- It ended the teen idol craze of the late '50s and early '60s.
- It cut short the Surf music wave that dominated the airwaves from 1962 to 1964.
- It cemented the definition for Rock 'n' Roll music to be based on electric guitars and drums.
- It shone the spotlight on the talents of singer-songwriters creating a more personal perception of the bands. It was no longer a songwriter factory throwing a new song over the wall for a band to record.

---

[20] Only Gary Lewis and the Playboys' "Count Me In" as Number 2 on the list held off a sweep.

Books:	*My British Invasion* Harold Bronson (Rare Bird Books, 2017)
Video:	*Casey Kasem's Rock n' Roll Goldmine - The British Invasion* (Standing Room Only, 2004)
Listen to:	*You Really Got Me* The Kinks (Pye, 1964)
	She's Not There The Zombies (Decca/Parrot, 1964)
	I'm Into Something Good Herman's Hermits (MGM/Columbia, 1964)
	House of the Rising Sun The Animals (Columbia Graphophone, 1964)

Psychedelic Rock

The development of Psychedelic Rock started in the mid-1960s in an effort to recreate the feeling from the use of LSD[21] and other hallucinogens. The music, like the drug, was intended to detach the listener from reality. Seeing a Psychedelic band in the mid-to-late '60s generally included a light show attempting to mimic the visual experience of an acid trip. The British interpretation resulted in Pop-psychedelia, which is a bit more whimsical in nature and the American interpretation was the harder "Acid Rock," which was predominantly west coast based.

The two albums generally given credit as the earliest Psychedelic albums by a major artist were The Beatles' *Revolver* and The Beach Boys' *Pet Sounds*[22] using trippy and drug-related lyrics. The Beach Boys' use of a Theremin[23] for *Good Vibrations* proved to be the catalyst needed to inspire

---

[21] Lysergic Acid Diethylamide (also referred to as "acid"). LSD and Psychedelic Rock were tightly linked to the counterculture revolution of the '60s.

[22] The Beach Boys helped usher in Psychedelia? Well, yes. Brian Wilson's masterpiece experimented on many levels including the use of sound effects and unconventional instruments. It was not a Psychedelic Rock album, but it laid the framework that would be used for subsequent Acid Rock bands.

[23] An interesting instrument consisting of two metal antennas that sense the relative position of the operator's hands. One hand controls the frequency (pitch) and the other controls the amplitude (volume). Used for the opening theme of the TV show *Star Trek*.

trips around the world. At this time, many advocates of the counterculture were congregating in the San Francisco area where the legends of Psychedelia formed. The most hard-core of these were those fans following the Grateful Dead (referred to as "Dead Heads"). They would still be following them around the country 40+ years later. The other major Psychedelic bands included Jefferson Airplane, Country Joe and the Fish, and Pink Floyd.

Grateful Dead

Pink Floyd

Books:	*Psychedelia: 101 Iconic Underground Rock Albums 1966–1970* Richard Morton Jack (Sterling, 2017)
Video:	*Rockin' at the Red Dog: The Dawn of Psychedelic Rock* (Monterey Video/Sunset Home Visual Entertainment, 2005)
Listen to:	*White Rabbit* Jefferson Airplane (RCA Victor, 1967)
	Purple Haze The Jimi Hendrix Experience (Track/Reprise, 1967)
	The End The Doors (Elektra, 1967)
	In-A-Gadda-Da-Vida Iron Butterfly (Atco, 1968)

Hard Rock

Hard Rock relies on guitar power chords and riffs to hit the listener straight in the gut. It also initiated the mainstream use of distortion and feedback to the delight of air guitar players worldwide. Leading the charge into the 1960's Hard Rock space were The Who, The Kinks, Deep Purple, and Led Zeppelin. Initially simple three-chord songs with increased distortion, the songs, as well as the abilities of the studios they were recorded in, became more sophisticated. Led Zeppelin's first two albums, released in 1969, show a quantum leap in sophistication of songwriting and creativeness using all that the studio's technology had to offer.

Robert Plant and Jimmy Page from Led Zeppelin

Listen to: ***Led Zeppelin I & II*** albums by Led Zeppelin (Atlantic, 1969)
Sunshine of Your Love Cream (Reaction, 1967)
My Generation The Who (Brunswick/Decca, 1965)
Summertime Blues Blue Cheer (Phillips, 1967)
Born to be Wild Steppenwolf (Dunhill/RCA, 1968)

70'S ROCK

While the '50s and '60s are viewed as the pioneer period for Rock, it's the 1970s where Rock's long-term viability was readily apparent and new pioneers were ready to take things into new and exciting directions. Each splinter faction felt like they were starting fresh and leaving the geezers behind[24].

Hard Rock

Hard Rock blossomed in the '70s and was more accepted into the mainstream, bringing us bands like Blue Öyster Cult, Ted Nugent, AC/DC, Rush, and Van Halen. During the early '60s, most indoor concerts were held in smaller venues. The mainstreaming of Hard Rock music made the '70s the decade of Arena Rock. Now instead of playing for 3,000-5,000 fans, arenas were used to accommodate 15,000+ fans. Stadium tours also proliferated around the world with crowds of 60,000+.

Angus Young of AC/DC

David Lee Roth of Van Halen

Books:	***Never a Dull Moment: 1971 The Year That Rock Exploded*** David Hepworth (Henry Holt and Co., 2016)
Listen to:	***Performance Rockin' the Fillmore*** Humble Pie (A&M, 1971)
	Machine Head Deep Purple (Warner Bros., 1972)
	Highway to Hell AC/DC (Albert/Atlantic, 1979)

---

[24] Little did they know that Geezer Rock would still be thriving over 45 years later.

Progressive Rock

The late '60s and early '70s saw the merging of Classical music with Rock to the delight of some and the horror of others. The "Progressive" title implies that the artists were trying to break the molds of the past and elevate the credibility of Rock to a larger audience. Bands such as Yes, Electric Light Orchestra, Renaissance, Moody Blues, Kansas, and Genesis produced complex albums that incorporated Classical roots and told themed stories in the fashion of an opera libretto.

Progressive Rock created a divide among Rock fans who either loved it or hated it. The haters generally considered it over-produced and pompous[25] while those who appreciated it tended to be very vocal. By the mid-'70s, fans grew tired of epic, extended songs. Some bands, such as Genesis, had major lineup changes leading to different directions. There is a strong correlation between Progressive and Punk Rock. Both wanted to advance music and reject commercialism. Some Progressive Rock albums are still heralded as classics today, but many were pushed to the back of the record store bins and faded away.

Genesis (with Peter Gabriel)

---

[25] Often referred to as "Nerd" rock for the Dungeons & Dragons enthusiasts.

Books:	***The Show That Never Ends: The Rise and Fall of Prog Rock***
	Dave Weigel (W. W. Norton & Company, 2017)
Listen to:	Albums:
	Eldorado Yes (Warner Bros./United Artists, 1974)
	Dark Side of the Moon Pink Floyd (Harvest, 1973)
	Close to the Edge Yes (Atlantic, 1972)
	Thick as a Brick Jethro Tull (Chrysalis/Reprise, 1972)
	Brain Salad Surgery Emerson, Lake and Palmer (Manicore, 1973)
	Leftoverture Kansas (Kirshner, 1976)

Heavy Metal

There is a blurry line between Hard Rock and Heavy Metal and by the late '70s the terms were almost interchangeable. Those better trained in music theory than I claim that Hard Rock uses R&B scales whereas Heavy Metal uses Classical scales. My definition of Heavy Metal (a.k.a. "Metal") builds on Hard Rock's power chords/riffs, which I assume to be the R&B influence, and rolls in greater sound distortion/ feedback along with an expositional increase in speed, intensity, and volume.

The Beatles helped jumpstart Metal with songs like "Helter Skelter," and bands like Steppenwolf, Cream, and Grand Funk[26] helped shape the Heavy Metal style of the early '70s. The Jimi Hendrix Experience's song, "Purple Haze," is thought to be the earliest Heavy Metal hit, but it was the release of Black Sabbath's self-titled debut album on Friday the 13th of February 1970 that defined Heavy Metal music as we know it today. Tony Iommi's[27] bone-crushing chords

---

[26] This band started out as "Grand Funk Railroad" and later changed their name to "Grand Funk." I assume they had problems fitting the whole name on the bass drum.

[27] Tony lost the tips of his middle and ring finger in an industrial accident as a teenager. Despite the ongoing pain, Tony made some thimbles for his fingers and adapted his playing style. The rest is Rock 'n' Roll history.

forever changed the Rock guitar landscape, and other bands, such as Deep Purple, Humble Pie, and Steppenwolf had their own Metal variations with great success. Most critics were dismissive of Metal bands, but the more that appeared, the more popular the genre grew.

Black Sabbath

Books:	***The Encyclopedia of Heavy Metal*** Daniel Bukszpan (Sterling, 2012)
Video:	***Metal - A Headbanger's Journey*** (Warner Bros., 2007)
Listen to:	Albums:
	Black Sabbath Black Sabbath (Warner Bros., 1970)
	Paranoid Black Sabbath (Warner Bros., 1970)
	Master of Reality Black Sabbath (Warner Bros., 1971)
	Vol. 4 Black Sabbath (Warner Bros., 1972)
	Sabbath Bloody Sabbath Black Sabbath (Warner Bros., 1973)
	Sabotage Black Sabbath (World Wide Artists, 1975)
	Sad Wings Of Destiny Judas Priest (Koch Records, 2000)

Glam/Glitter Rock

Glitter Rock seemed like more of a fashion than a genre of music, but once you look at the standout Glitter bands, such as T. Rex, Slade, Mott the Hoople, and the New York Dolls, you feel that the song and stage fashion styles go hand in hand with glamour, theatrics, and mysticism as the center themes.

The epitome of Glitter Rock was David Bowie who, after putting out some interesting albums in the late '60s, launched a series of persona driven albums, with outfits to match. Albums such as *Ziggy Stardust and the Spiders from Mars* and *Aladdin Sane* brought out the performance artist in Bowie who successfully reinvented himself several times over his career.

David Bowie

Books:	*Shock and Awe: Glam Rock and Its Legacy, from the Seventies to the Twenty-first Century* Simon Reynolds (Dey Street Books, 2016)
Video:	*Ziggy Stardust and The Spiders From Mars* (Parlophone, 2003)
Listen to:	*All the Young Dudes* Mott the Hoople (Columbia, 1972)
	Cum On Feel the Noize Slade (Polydor, 1973)
	Trash New York Dolls (Mercury, 1973)
	Something for the Girl with Everything Sparks (Island, 1974)

Punk

Tommy Ramone, the drummer for the Ramones is quoted as saying, "In its initial form, a lot of [1960's] stuff was innovative and exciting. Unfortunately, what happens is that people who could not hold a candle to the likes of Hendrix started noodling away. Soon you had endless solos that went nowhere. By 1973, I knew that what was needed was some pure, stripped down, no bullshit Rock 'n' Roll."

Drawing from the Garage Bands that remained under the mainstream radar in the late '60s and early '70s, such as MC5, the Stooges, and The Velvet Underground, Punk Rock exploded in the U.S. in the mid-'70s with the Ramones, Television, and Johnny Thunders and the Heartbreakers. In the U.K., Punk rose out of the economic depression and an all-time unemployment high featuring the most infamous Punk Rock band, the Sex Pistols and their lead singer Johnny Rotten. Even though they produced only one album and four singles in their short two-and-a-half-year history, they are regarded as one of the most influential bands from the '70s, for their attitude as well as their music.

Punk seemed to flounder during the '80s, but in the '90s saw the rise of bands like Green Day and The Offspring bring it back to center. The cycle of Punk is clear.

1. A faction decides that things are getting too commercial and sophisticated.
2. They cut the music and production back to the bare essentials.
3. The fans embrace the change making them a success.
4. The cycle restarts.

The cycle seems to take 10-15 years and currently bands like G.L.O.S.S., Destruction Unit, and RVIVR continuing the proud tradition.

The Ramones

Books:	***Please Kill Me: The Uncensored Oral History of Punk*** McNeil/McCain (Grove Press, 2016)
Video:	***Punk – Attitude*** (Capitol Entertainment, 2005)
Listen to:	***New Rose*** The Damned (Stiff, 1976)
	On the Run Eddie and the Hot Rods (Island, 1976)
	Anarchy in the UK Sex Pistols (EMI, 1976)
	I Wanna Be Sedated Ramones (Sire, 1978)
	London Calling The Clash (CBS, 1979)

New Wave

New Wave, also referred to as "Alternative Rock," is considered a meaningless term by some music historians. For the purposes of this book its definition is the music from the mid-'70s to the early '80s where bands adopted the mindset of Punk, but placed a much stronger emphasis on musicianship and an increased complexity of songs. This return to strong basics was a response to the stadium spectacles and the over-production of Progressive Rock. New Wave songs tended to use fast, choppy, rhythm guitar riffs and incorporated keyboards. Early New Wave standouts were the Talking Heads, Elvis Costello, Devo, The Cars, and Blondie.

I mark the end of New Wave by the start of the video music era, even though some bands continued to thrive. The primary reason for this separation is the changes in their songwriting to accommodate the new visual medium.

Elvis Costello

Talking Heads

Books:	*The Encyclopedia of New Wave* Daniel Bukszpan (Sterling, 2012)
Listen to:	*Love is the Drug* Roxy Music (EG, 1975)
	Psycho Killer Talking Heads (Sire, 1977)
	Watching the Detectives Elvis Costello (Stiff, 1977)
	Walking on the Moon The Police (A&M/AMS, 1979)

ROCK IN THE VIDEO AGE

W hen Music Television (MTV) played their first music video—*Music Killed the Radio Star* by The Buggles—on August 1, 1981, it was the start of a major shift in how music was made, sold, and performed. There are examples of music videos (a.k.a. "filmed inserts," "illustrated songs," and "promotional clips") prior to 1981 such as The Moody Blues' *Go Now*, The Who's *Happy Jack*, and The Beatles' *Strawberry Fields Forever/Penny Lane* videos. Queen's 1975 *Bohemian Rhapsody* video is regarded as the first global hit where a video was part of the designed promotion and David Bowie's 1980's *Ashes to Ashes* video (one of the first experimental, avant-garde Rock 'n' Roll videos), but without an outlet to play and replay the videos, there was no motivation to incur the expense. That all changed when MTV came on the air, playing music videos 24 hours a day, seven days a week. The vacuum of available videos necessitated a lot of repeats, but once the music companies jumped in, there was no turning back.

Videos were introduced by Video Jockeys (VJs), with celebrity VJs such as Billy Idol and Eddie Murphy. Artists saw the music video as an extension of their creative options. Some videos were straight musical performances, but the most popular were those that told stories, included eye-popping visuals, and of course, had good old-fashioned sex appeal.

The video story didn't always line up with the song, but no one really cared as long as it garnered attention. Artists started considering the music video as part of the song creation process and many artists, such as Duran Duran and Madonna, owe much of their success to music videos.

Record companies saw an immediate impact on sales for those bands who were being featured on MTV and adjusted their strategies to ensure that music videos were a part of the album preview/release process. This naturally led to excess with over-produced videos for boring or just plain bad songs.

A sister channel, Video Hits 1 (VH1) was launched in an attempt to capture an older demographic. In 1989, the MTV Unplugged show was launched. It was generally used for bands to play an acoustic greatest hits set until Nirvana upended things by playing some deep tracks that set the bar much higher for later shows.

One of the biggest moments in MTV history was the premiere of Michael Jackson's 14-minute *Thriller* video on December 2, 1983. Up to this point, MTV did not play many black artists, stating that it was difficult to find African-American artists who fit the channel's format. *Thriller* broke this barrier, opening the floodgates for other artists of color such as Prince, Stevie Wonder, and Chaka Khan. For the rest of the '80s and up to the mid-'90s, MTV made and broke bands by playing their videos, or not. By the late '90s, the novelty of a music video station had run its course with new, non-music shows consuming 35% of the air time. By 2008, streaming videos over the internet made static play schedules obsolete and MTV reduced its music video time to only three hours per day.

Michael Jackson

In the midst of music in the video age, music genres developing in the '60s and '70s blossomed in the '80s. Many New Wave artists thrived, Rap took off, but it was the big Hair Bands, often referred to as Glam Metal, that ruled with our ozone paying the price via thousands of hair spray cans being used to hold hair up for the sake of Rock 'n' Roll. With many elements of Glitter Rock merged with Heavy Metal riffs, soaring guitar solos and an attitude for excess, bands such as Mötley Crüe, Poison, and Bon Jovi dominated MTV and album sales. The age of Hair bands lasted into the early '90s where all of the Glam started to feel contrary to the heart of Metal. A huge backlash was about to strike and upend everything – again.

Books: *I Want My MTV: The Uncensored Story of the Music Video Revolution* Tannenbaum/Marks (Plume, 2012)

Listen to: *MTV Unplugged in New York* album by Nirvana (DGC, 1994)

GRUNGE

In the late '80s, a sound emerged in the Pacific Northwest that combined Punk, '60's Garage Rock, and stripped down Heavy Metal. The heavy bass line, distorted guitars, and socially conscious lyrics defined the Grunge genre that ended the redundancy of the big Hair era, making bands like Nirvana, Pearl Jam, and Soundgarden household names. The emergence of Grunge is generally credited to the isolation of the Northwest music market and organic growth of a style using a Punk attitude, a love of Pop's catchy riffs, and low tech recording technologies[28]. Many bands pasted with the Grunge moniker resented the association.

The story of Grunge is both a happy and sad one. Its happy portion centers around a counter-culture movement that thrived while being ignored by the recording industry that was focused on Los Angeles and New York big Hair bands.

Some historians tie Neil Young's distorted guitar on his *Rust Never Sleeps*[29] album as a rallying point for Grunge. The Sub Pop record label was the primary reason Grunge made it beyond a local sound. They were responsible for the marketing of the "Seattle Sound" to the world as well as the descriptor "Grunge"[30]. One of the many perceptions of the Grunge image included the "thrift shop" look which resulted in a sales explosion of plaid shirts and black work boots.

The sad part of the Grunge story is how the record labels converged on the Seattle area to cash in on its popularity, signing just about anyone. They also marketed other bands, not related to the Seattle area by location or sound, as being Grunge. Nirvana had been a relatively unknown punkish band that changed their lineup, hit their songwriting stride, and got the perfect producer (Butch Vig) with an amazing synergy that produced the album *Nevermind*. The first single off the album was "Smells Like Teen Spirit," which helped throw the Grunge genre into high gear with the term being misapplied to anything remotely Metal. Nirvana ended up being a double-edged sword for Grunge. It was the reason it became a

---

[28] Nirvana's debut album, *Bleach*, was recorded at a cost of $606.17.
[29] This is an album that everyone interested in the history of Rock should be well acquainted with. The opening songs use a delicate, acoustic guitar, with the sound becoming harder as the album progresses. By the time you get to the final track, "Hey Hey, My My (Into the Black)," a feedback-filled thrashing guitar is used to great effect.
[30] While the originator of the term is hotly contested, there is no doubt as to Sub Pop's role in its success.

worldwide craze, but it was also the reason it ultimately faded away with Kurt Cobain's death.

Books:	***Everybody Loves Our Town: An Oral History of Grunge*** Mark Yarm (Three Rivers Press, 2012)
Video:	***Nirvana: Live at the Paramount*** (Geffen, 2012)
Listen to:	Albums:
	Nevermind Nirvana (Geffen, 1991)
	Ten Pearl Jam (Epic, 1991)
	Superunknown Soundgarden (A&M, 1994)

HEAVY METAL IN THE '80S, '90S, AND BEYOND

Heavy Metal music boomed in the '90s, but as part of this boom, it also splintered into many different factions. The term "Heavy Metal" had become too broad to adequately describe the music being released and many sub-genres were defined.

Classic/Traditional Metal

Geezer Rock lives as Black Sabbath, AC/DC, Judas Priest, Iron Maiden and others continue to draw listeners and crowds. It is, by far, the most mainstream form of Heavy Metal and does not show any signs of weakening.

Mötley Crüe

Listen to:	Albums:
	Brave New World Iron Maiden (EMI/Portrait/Columbia, 2000)
	AEnima Tool (Zoo Entertainment, 1996)

Thrash Metal

The Thrash title is an appropriate description for guitar style used in this genre (low register riffs and metal-shredding solos). Originating as an antithesis to the Glam/Hair rock of the '80s, Thrash Metal bands like Metallica, Slayer, Anthrax, and Megadeath were initially overshadowed by the Grunge movement, but hung on and persevered in the '90s and '00s.

Purists believe that Metallica's "Black" album was the start of their turn away from Thrash, but it also drew in fans and brought more attention to established bands such as Pantera.

Slayer

Listen to: Albums:

Metallica (a.k.a. The Black Album) Metallica (Electra, 1991)

Vulgar Display of Power Pantera (Atco, 1992)

Death Metal

Death Metal represents the stereotypical outsider's view of Heavy Metal: dark, ominous, and foreboding – and let's not forget scary (especially to parents). Listen at your own peril[31]. Never reaching mainstream status, Death Metal has had some mild success with bands like Cannibal Corpse and Morbid Angel.

Listen to:	***Tomb of the Mutilated*** album by Cannibal Corpse (Metal Blade, 1992)

Cannibal Corpse

---

[31] If that warning does not get your inner child to want to listen to Death Metal, nothing will.

Speed Metal

Taking the core Heavy Metal concepts and infusing Punk-inspired speed, Speed Metal is a wonder to behold, both to listen to and watch live. Deep Purple's "Fireball"[32] and Queen's "Stone Cold Crazy" are songs pointed to as early influences. The first band classified as true Speed Metal was Motörhead who helped pioneer techniques still used today to play at a fierce, non-stop tempo.

Listen to: **Ace of Spades** album by Motörhead (Mercury, 1980)

Lemmy Kilmister from Motörhead

---

[32] Worth a listen just for drummer Ian Paice's drumming.

Others

There are many other sub-genres including Post-Metal, Power Metal, Latin Metal, Industrial Metal, Folk Metal, Funk Metal, Neoclassical Metal, Metalcore and more. Take a look at them all. There's something for everyone!

SHOCK ROCK

S hock Rock is not a musical genre, but a live performance style that has its roots in the 1950s. Alan Freed, as part of his Rock 'n' Roll roadshow, paid Screamin' Jay Hawkins to emerge from a coffin onstage among smoke and flashes. Screamin' embraced the response, adding bones coming out of his nose, singing with a rubber snake around his neck, waving a skull on a stick (named "Henry" – which he occasionally set on fire) and brandishing a spear. When Screamin' went on tour to support his *Feast of the Mau Mau* album, he had a large cauldron on stage to which he added mannequin limbs and poured in containers of red goo (ketchup). While never achieving significant commercial success, his contributions to the world of entertainment is undeniable.

Next up is Arthur Brown who had a hit single with the song "Fire" that begins with him yelling "I am the God of Hell Fire!" with his powerful four-octave voice. He also used face makeup that inspired Alice Cooper, and wore flamboyant, over-the-top theatrical outfits. Oh, yeah... he also had a burning metal helmet on his head as he sang. This level of theatrics would not even raise an eyebrow today, but in 1967, it seemed outright evil. Jimi Hendrix loved Arthur and his music and promoted him every chance he got.

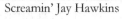
Screamin' Jay Hawkins   Arthur Brown

In September of 1964, The Who was playing a gig in England. During the performance, Pete Townshend accidentally broke the neck of his beloved Rickenbacker guitar. His initial reaction was sadness in that something he deemed precious was gone. The sadness changed to anger when the audience didn't seem to care or understand that it was a sad event. He then made a big show of destroying the rest of the guitar, picking up a replacement, and playing on. Pete went on to destroy many more guitars, but only when he felt it was appropriate to the show. He never wanted to be predictable.

Many artists have destroyed their guitars over the years, such as Richie Blackmore and Kurt Cobain and it still remains an exciting part of a Rock 'n' Roll show. The Who's drummer, Keith Moon, famously overloaded the explosives in his drum kit for their U.S. TV debut on the *Smothers Brothers Comedy Hour*. At the climax of the song "My Generation," he blew up the kit along with one of Pete's eardrums. Other casualities of the explosion were show guest Bette Davis, who fainted, Tommy Smothers' acoustic guitar (which Pete smashed after he walked out at the end of the song), and Moon himself who sustained shrapnel cuts from his cymbals.

Pete Townshend   Keith Moon

The undisputed Godfather of Shock Rock is Alice Cooper. He wore heavy makeup inspired by the movie *What Ever Happened to Baby Jane?* and tattered clothing with thigh-high, leopard-spotted, platform boots. The shock element came about very innocently when, somehow, a chicken found its way onstage. Alice, with zero farmyard experience, reasoned that if chickens have wings, they must be able to fly (they can't). He lofted the chicken into the audience and it came down into the first few rows where the crowd reportedly tore the bird to pieces. The publicity from the non-intentional stunt made the band a recognizable name and fueled many urban legends such as Alice killing the bird himself and drinking the blood. As the popularity grew, so did the stage theatrics. They simulated electric chair and hanging executions and added a live boa constrictor named Yvonne writhing on Alice as he sang.

The 1973 *Billion Dollar Babies* tour pulled out all the stops with a show climax of Alice being beheading by guillotine. I have the good fortune of being friends with James "The Amazing" Randi who designed and built the guillotine as well as acting as the on-stage executioner for Alice. Randi relates that each night, as he waited with Alice at the base of the stage steps, they went through a fixed routine. Randi would prepare hand flashers that would shoot a stack of flame and, when ready, position them in Alice's hands. As the rest of the band climbed the stage, Alice would close his eyes and start taking deep breaths with sporadic body shaking for 30 seconds or so. When his eyes opened, Randi could see that the friendly, gentle man he had spent hours with on the road, at the hotel, in the limo to the event, and in the dressing room was gone. The character Alice Cooper had arrived. Randi watched him climb the steps to the stage, hoping the flashers did not go off prematurely, and watched the character stagger to the center of the stage, set off the flashers, one by one, and hold sway over the audience until the show was over.

The larger the stage, the larger the bands needed to be. Large sets, stage props, and over-the-top light shows became the norm for most arena and stadium tours in the '70s. Pink Floyd used giant inflatable pigs. ZZ Top used a buffalo, longhorn steer, venomous rattlesnakes, some tarantulas, and six vultures on stage. KISS's early theatrics included fire-breathing, fake blood spitting, smoking guitars, and a drum kit that rose several feet into the air. By the time of their 1976 *Destroyer* tour, the stage had an apocalyptic theme that included multiple levels, hydraulic lifts to carry the artists to dizzying heights, confetti machines to snow paper on the audience, and fire stacks that could warm the back row. There were some holdouts to the stripped-down approach such as Peter Frampton and The Kinks, but as the cost of putting on an arena or stadium show rose, so did ticket prices and the expectations of the buyer.

Alice Cooper

Alice with snake

There have been a myriad of bands using foul language, controversial lyrics, and onstage theatrics to try to be noticed. Noteworthy Shock Rock bands include:

- GWAR – Choosing a detailed science-fiction based theme for their stage show with each character a unique interplanetary warrior, GWAR continues with the theme in their music where they frequently include political satire. The music, the spectacle, and spraying their audience with various fluids representing blood, urine, and semen brings the faithful back again and again.

- Slayer – As one of the early Thrash Metal bands, Slayer looked and sounded dangerous (especially to parents), generating lawsuits, album bans, and criticism for their music and performances but always insisted that the music came first and the stage show second. They are cited as a major influence for a plethora of Heavy Metal bands.

- Marilyn Manson – Using the first name of iconic female sex symbol and the last name of iconic serial killers to develop unique band member names, Marilyn Manson took full advantage of surrealist and grotesque imagery for their music videos. Critics claim that their success was solely due to the videos and they could not have succeeded on their music alone.

- Rob Zombie – Starting with the band White Zombie and then going solo, Rob incorporated themes, storylines, and even sound clips of classic horror movies in his work. Not content conquering the stage, Rob also directs horror movies including *House of 1000 Corpses, The Devil's Rejects,* and 2 *Halloween* series reboots.

- Slipknot – Classified as a Nu Metal band, Slipknot features the pyrotechnics and stagecraft of KISS taken to the next level. Each band member wears a unique mask and outfit and are referred to by a number based on their role (zero through 8). Accused of using masks as a gimmick, the band maintains they use masks to divert attention from themselves and allow the focus to be on the music.

GWAR

Rob Zombie

Slipknot

Books:	***Shock Rock I & II*** Jeff Gelb (Pocket Books, 1992 and 1994)
Listen to:	***Billion Dollar Babies*** album by Alice Cooper (Warner Bros., 1973)
	Dragula Rob Zombie (Geffen, 1998)
	Antichrist Superstar Marilyn Manson (Nothing, Interscope, 1996)
	Vlad the Impaler GWAR (Metal Blade Records, 1990)

ELVIS

Elvis is truly the King of Rock 'n' Roll. Yes, he was a teen idol. Yes, he initially sang in the Rockabilly format, but his place in Rock history is more deeply rooted. His melding of Blues, Country, and Gospel puts him right at the start of what we call Rock 'n' Roll today. He had a beautiful voice with a larger than two-octave range that most considered pitch perfect. He came off as a true rebel. His hair was long, he swiveled his hips, and was hated by all parents. What could possibly draw a teenager in more than that? People who dismiss Elvis are missing out on the core history of Rock. Don't be one of these people. Elvis' career went through six stages.

Early Elvis

Elvis had been told he was no singer many times before he walked into Sam Phillips' Sun studios in 1953. Even then, he recorded several songs that no one liked. It was not until during a break between recordings with some studio musicians in 1954 that the magic occurred.

"All of a sudden, Elvis just got started singing this song, jumping around and acting the fool, and then Bill picked up his bass and started acting the fool, too, and I started playing with them. Sam had the door to the control room open and stuck his neck out. 'What are you doing?' he asked. 'We don't know,' we said. 'Well, back up, try to find a place to start, and do it again'."

~Scotty Moore, Elvis' guitar player

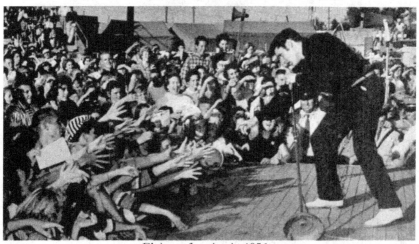

Elvis performing in 1956

"That's Alright Mama" was the first big regional hit for Elvis. In 1955, he signed on with Colonel Tom Parker as his manager, who quickly got him signed with RCA. Both 1956 and 1957 were banner years for Elvis:

- He had his first number one hit with "Heartbreak Hotel."
- His self-titled debut album was the first Rock 'n' Roll record to top the Billboard charts and then held it for ten weeks.
- He appeared twice on *The Milton Berle Show*.
- He appeared on *The Steve Allen Show* (where he sang "Hound Dog" to a basset hound).
- He appeared on *The Ed Sullivan Show* three times. During the third appearance, the cameramen were instructed to only film him "from the waist up."

Up until 1958, Elvis had acted in a few movies and had dreams of becoming a serious actor, but Uncle Sam threw up a detour that neither Elvis nor the Colonel could make go away.

Service Elvis

Elvis was drafted into the army in March of 1958. At this point, he was one of the most famous persons in the world of entertainment. Many parents rejoiced at the thought of this evil, hip-swiveling menace to society being out of the spotlight, and figured he would never be in the limelight again. Elvis was given the opportunity to serve in the Special Services where he would entertain the troops and receive priority housing, but instead chose to serve as a regular soldier, going where they needed him and gaining the respect of many Americans, including the parents who had hated him.

Elvis' mother died before he finished his training. This was a severe blow to him, and the imagined guilt of being somehow responsible stayed with him for the rest of his life.

Elvis was shipped to Germany for the remainder of his service where he was assigned the task of being a driver. He kept his head down for his two years of service and was generally liked by his unit. He demonstrated his generosity by donating his Army pay to charity, buying television sets for the entire post, and purchasing an extra set of fatigues for everyone in his unit. He attained the rank of sergeant before his discharge in March of 1960. Oh, he also met a 14-year-old girl, named Priscilla Beaulieu, which he took a shine to. He would spend over seven years courting her.

Elvis was welcomed back to the U.S. as a guest on Frank Sinatra's 1960 TV special. He was embraced by his fans as though he had never left.

Film Elvis

Colonel Parker had released, to great success, songs Elvis had recorded before going into the service, but that well had run dry and more material was needed. After some initial recording sessions, Elvis spent the next seven years focusing on films and their soundtracks. He still hoped for the dramatic role that would silence his critics. During the 1960s, Elvis made 27 films. Some are worthwhile, but most were part of the Hollywood grist mill and were downright embarrassing. The forays into drama were not received well and he fell back onto the tried and true formula. Most films were panned by the critics, but were well attended by his fans who also purchased the soundtrack albums.

The successes continued but were slowly shrinking until 1967, which started as a good year for Elvis, when he married Priscilla, but his movies and their soundtrack sales had tanked and the Colonel had trouble getting studios interested in future projects. Record companies also thought that his star had faded. The failures of 1967 were a wakeup call to Elvis, the Colonel, and the record/movie companies. Elvis swore he would never sing another song, for the rest of his life, that he did not believe in.

Elvis and Juliet Prowse
in *G.I. Blues*

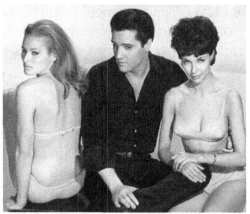

Elvis with Ursula Andress and Elsa Cárdenas
in *Fun in Acapulco*

Come-Back Elvis

Elvis and the Colonel decided it was time for a return to TV, the first time since 1960. They brokered a deal where Elvis would have a Christmas television special. The Colonel's vision was to have him sing some Christmas carols and feature a few guests. Elvis had an entirely different idea: large production numbers interspersed with live music segments performed in the round with a small stage and a few musicians. Dressed in black leather pants and jacket, Elvis joked with the audience and told stories in between songs. The show was broadcast December 3, 1968, and was the highest-rated television special of the year. Elvis' star may have faded before the comeback special, but now looked brighter than ever.

Vegas Elvis

The success of the TV special made negotiations for Elvis to appear in Las Vegas easy. While the money and interest were present, Elvis was a bit apprehensive. He remembered bombing there in 1956 and that memory haunted him right up until the opening on July 31, 1969, at the Las Vegas International Hotel. Even though he was then 34 years old, Elvis had no problem bringing the same energy as the 21-year-old Elvis. The audiences loved it and the 29 shows over a one-month engagement set new records for attendance (101,509) and gross ($1,522,635). Las Vegas had found its new King.

Elvis meeting President Nixon in 1970

Elvis Forever

Elvis returned to Vegas for 14 more engagements, earning the title of the most successful big name act to ever play there. In the first half of the '70s, his concert and record production was running at a high, almost dangerous, level. From 1969 to his death, Elvis performed 1,126 shows and each year, he would release 2-3 studio albums, a couple of live albums, and several singles. Sometime in the 1960s, Elvis started taking amphetamines and diet pills to control his weight, which ultimately led to a sleeping problem he tried to solve with sleeping pills. Add in some pain pills and the grind of touring/recording, and you end up with a lethal mix that killed the King on August 16, 1977. Though he never toured outside the U.S., the entire world mourned.

Elvis and his parents are buried at his Graceland mansion

There are many legends around Elvis' excesses that, while rooted in truth, are exaggerated to the point of being silly. During his final year of touring, the quality of his performances suffered, including the show I attended with Bruce Springsteen[33] in Philadelphia on May 28, 1977. It was a mixed feeling actually laying eyes on the King with some of the Elvis charm and the power of his voice coming through, but also a bit sad to see the overweight Elvis go through the motions with pain rather than energy or enthusiasm. A 40-year-old memory has him saying, "I know you have heard a lot about me, but as long as I have my voice and my health, to hell with the rest."

Elvis was far from perfect and he was definitely taken advantage of by his manager and many others. He also was the spark of a music revolution that I assume, since you are reading this book, has profoundly affected the music you listen to and enjoy. Take the time to root through the films and

---

[33] "The Boss" and I didn't go together, sit together, or even see each other. I only found out 35 years later that he and Miami Steve were at the concert as well. He has been quoted on how disappointed he was with the show.

records he produced and find the magical ones that helped make the world a better place for people like you and me. The King lives! Long live the King!

Books:	*Elvis* Dave Marsh (Smithmark Pub, 1997)
Video:	*Elvis: That's the Way It Is* (Warner Bros., 1970)
	Viva Las Vegas (MGM, 1964)
Listen to:	*Elvis* (RCA, 1956)
	Elvis: 30 #1 Hits (RCA, 2002)

THE BEATLES

Paul McCartney, John Lennon, George Harrison, and Ringo Starr were the catalyst for a revolution in music not seen before or since. A significant reason The Beatles are held in such high regard is the context in which they appeared. For those who did not experience The Beatles phenomena[34], it is a difficult context to convey, but I will do my best. Rock 'n' Roll emerged in the '50s thanks to Elvis, Chuck Berry, and many other pioneers. By the early '60s, Elvis was into his movie phase, radio was dominated by Pop, and TV had token musical appearances on shows like *Ed Sullivan* ("And now here's something for the kiddies!"). Other important parts of this context:

- At the time, singing and songwriting seemed to be mutually exclusive with many songwriters tucked away in L.A. or New York City offices cranking out great songs that many yearned to record for themselves, but due to the record companies' control of everything, had to throw them over the wall to the performers.

- Performers put out an album per year with singles being slowly released from them over 9-12 months to maintain album sales. One or two successful singles per album was the norm, with the rest of the tracks generally considered filler.

- With few exceptions, artists served under the will of the record company who made every decision regarding the artist's career.

The Beginning

There were two major players who guided The Beatles to success. The first was record shop manager Brian Epstein. He had heard some of the buzz about the group and decided to see their noon concert at the Cavern Club in November of 1961[35]. He decided to manage the group and transformed them from wearing leather jackets and jeans to suits and ties. He

---

34 Known as Beatlemania, the fan frenzy had never been seen before.

35 Afterwards Brian Epstein said, "I was immediately struck by their music, their beat and their sense of humour on stage — and, even afterwards, when I met them, I was struck again by their personal charm."

molded their on-stage personas, including the synchronized bow at the end of songs, and oversaw the removal of drummer Pete Best and the insertion of Ringo Starr as they started to record. Without Epstein's guidance, it is very likely we never would have heard of The Beatles.

Brian Epstein

The Beatles with George Martin

The second major player in The Beatles' career was producer George Martin. While his experience had been Classical music and comedy records, he thought Paul and John's voices promising. George was able to push all four members and pull out performances still heralded as classics today. Without the combination of Epstein and Martin, music history would be very different.

The Beatles released their first album, *Please Please Me*, in March of 1963. As they toured for the rest of the year, Beatlemania ramped up. Large, often hysterical, crowds greeted them at any appearance in public. In Plymouth, England, British police used high-pressure water hoses to control the crowd. In November, they released their second album, *With The Beatles*, which replaced their first album on the top of the charts after 30 weeks. On the album sleeve, the text referred to them as the "fabulous foursome" which the media shortened to "Fab Four."

Songs from both albums were not widely played or sold in the U.S. during 1963. Epstein arranged a marketing campaign that drove demand and the single, "I Want to Hold Your Hand," sold a million copies in the U.S. by January of 1964. When the Fab Four landed at New York's JFK airport, over 3000 screaming fans greeted them. On February 9, 1964, they appeared on *The Ed Sullivan Show* where they were watched by 73 million viewers in over 23 million households[36]. Most of the adults I heard complain were more upset about the band's long hair than their music. They played a few more concerts along with *The Ed Sullivan Show* a second time before heading back to England. During the first week of April 1964, 12 Beatles songs were listed on the Billboard Hot 100 singles chart, including the top five. Beatlemania had achieved a firm grip on the U.S. that still exists today.

The Beatles as they arrived in America on February 7, 1964

John and Paul's songwriting collaboration is the most successful in history. The duo had made an agreement, before

---

[36] I was one of those viewers. I was a five-year-old boy sitting on my mother's lap as she exclaimed over and over again, "Look at that hair!" and, "They will never last!"

becoming famous, to always share credit on Beatles' songs, even if written by only one of them. In many cases, one made only minor contributions to the other's song, but between 1962 and 1969, they both honored the agreement, publishing 180 songs with both receiving credit. The partnership also included a rivalry which drove both to constantly attempt to outdo the other, despite the shared credit.

Mid-'60s

In July of 1964, the movie *A Hard Day's Night* was released. This was a mock documentary of a day with the band as they prepared for a TV appearance. It was silly, as well as fun and the songs showed how the Lennon/McCartney songwriting team had matured. It was during this period that both Paul and John started being dismissive of George Harrison's songs during recording sessions, leading to resentment by George that would build over the years[37]. During the rest of 1964 and into 1965, more successful albums and their second movie, *Help!*, were released. The movie was designed as a spoof of James Bond and the huge success of its soundtrack. An August 15, 1965, concert at Shea Stadium kicked off the concept of stadium shows[38].

---

[37] Some historians argue that George Harrison's songs were much more complex and difficult to learn, leading to the dismissive attitude.
[38] The in-house public address system was used for amplification, resulting in a thin, tinny sound at best.

The Beatles were known for their horseplay

As the band entered the studio with George Martin in October of 1965, they wanted to make more than just a collection of singles. They wanted an album that would have meaning as a whole, resulting in *Rubber Soul*. Often held up as the pinnacle of their recording career, it showed even more maturity and complexity in the songwriting and greater confidence in their ability. Paul said, "We'd had our cute period, and now it was time to expand."

In June of 1966, Capitol Records released a compilation called *Yesterday and Today* containing songs not released in the U.S. from British albums. The cover of the album had the band, in white smocks, draped with meat and plastic baby dolls. The initial backlash from the cover was so great that Capitol ordered all jacket sheets to be destroyed and for those album sleeves that the sheet had already been applied, an alternate jacket sheet was applied over the offending one. Copies of the album with the alternate jacket are one of the most highly prized collectables in music history with mint copies, still in their shrink wrap, selling for over $125,000.

The Beatles playing in Rome

Studio vs. Live

The band's next album, *Revolver*, was released in August of 1966, showing the band's willingness to experiment with different styles, instruments, and studio effects. As the band prepared for the supporting tour, they felt they would not be able to effectively recreate the new songs live and did not use them in any of the tour's shows. This drew the line between "studio" Beatles and "live" Beatles.

Knowing that the screaming would be relentless at the shows, they attempted to use more powerful speakers, but it was not enough. The "studio" Beatles would win, at the expense of the "live" Beatles. On August 29, 1966, at Candlestick Park in San Francisco, The Beatles played their last commercial concert.

Sgt. Peppers

Freed from the rigors of touring, they became much more experimental with the creation of *Sgt. Pepper's Lonely Hearts Club Band*. They used studio equipment in odd ways, such as varying the speed of voices/instruments, and utilized a 40-

piece orchestra. Paul suggested that the album should represent a performance by their Sgt. Pepper alter egos. The resulting album was a triumph melding Rock 'n' Roll, Pop, vaudeville, chamber, circus, music hall, and Indian classical music. Most artists were amazed at how such a complex album was recorded using only four tracks. The album cover was groundbreaking as well. It featured the band, in pseudo-military outfits, in front of life-sized cardboard cut-outs of 61 famous people including the "Fab Four" version of the group and has become one of the most imitated images in the world.

The album was the fastest selling album ever for The Beatles with 2.5 million sold in the first three months. It also appears that *Sgt. Peppers* was the beginning of the end for the group. George and Ringo both expressed frustration that the album creation process had become John and Paul layering on their desires without much playing together as a band.

On June 25, 1967, The Beatles performed "All You Need Is Love" to an estimated 350 million viewers over the first live global television broadcast. A couple months later, the band was introduced to Maharishi Mahesh Yogi. They traveled to a Transcendental Meditation retreat of the Maharishi's, but left early when they heard of their manager Brian Epstein's death. While ruled an accident, it was generally thought to be a suicide. His death shook the weakening foundations of the group.

Magical, White and Yellow

The next project the band focused on was the *Magical Mystery Tour* TV special which featured them riding around the countryside getting on and off a bus. The show was not well-liked, but the soundtrack was extremely popular and featured more psychedelic songs expected by fans. The group headed off to India for the Maharishi's three-month "guide" course. Ringo got bored, leaving after 10 days, and Paul left a few weeks later. John left with George two months in, after being convinced that the Maharishi was trying to manipulate them and that the Yogi was making sexual advances to female attendees[39].

During the recording of the *White* album, tension between bandmates was at an all-time high. Ringo quit, but returned after a two-week period, and John insisted that his newfound love, artist Yoko Ono, be present at all sessions despite a well-established understanding otherwise. This was the first album released under the new Beatles-owned label, Apple Records, and while the double album sold well and has many good songs, it felt too multipolar for many fans.

In June of 1968, the animated, psychedelic movie, *Yellow Submarine*, was released with not too great reviews. For some reason the soundtrack followed seven months later. The singles from the album were popular, but the album became one of the poorest selling in The Beatles' catalog.

Swan Song(s)

In January of 1969, they recorded (and filmed) most of the tracks for what would be the final Beatles album, *Let It Be*, with all members of the band remembering it as the worst of all their recording sessions. The resulting film showed their creative process around song development, but also some of the bickering among the band members. Billy Preston was brought in to play keyboards and lighten the mood and received credit on the "Get Back" single. He was the only musician to ever get that type of credit on a Beatles release. The second half of the film is the impromptu final concert on the roof of the Apple Records building during lunchtime on January 30, 1969.

---

[39] Paul remarked, "We made a mistake. We thought there was more to him than there was."

Beatles statue in Liverpool, England

Despite all of the issues from the *Let It Be* sessions, the group was back into the studio to record *Abbey Road*, which was released in September of 1969, six days after Lennon told the rest of the band that he was leaving the group. It sold 4 million copies in three months. The *Let It Be* recordings were turned over to Phil Spector who remixed and overdubbed significant portions of the songs, much to Paul's dismay, and he publicly announced his departure from the band on April 10, 1970. The *Let It Be* movie and album were released in May of 1970. There were motions to legally dissolve The Beatles' partnership (not finalized until 1974 due to legal disputes) and The Beatles were no more.

Things to Think About

For those of you still are not convinced that The Beatles were important, please consider the following statistics:

- 600 million albums sold worldwide with over 1.6 billion singles.
- Seven consecutive Number 1 albums.

- Their music has spent 1,278 weeks on the Billboard charts.
- They received 8 Grammy awards and 1 Academy Award for Best Original Movie Score (*Let It Be*).
- They are collectively included in *Time* magazine's compilation of the 20th Century's 100 most influential people.

All band members went on to create much more wonderful music in their solo careers, but The Beatles, as they recorded and performed between 1963 and 1969, left a profound mark on music, culture, and the lives of millions around the world.

Fans hoped for a reunion someday. NBC's *Saturday Night Live* producer, Lorne Michaels, went on the air April 24, 1976, making an offer of $3000 to the band to reunite on the show. The interesting thing is that Paul and John had since smoothed things over and were watching the show together with the rest of the world. They toyed with the idea of going down to collect half the money, but did not move on it. George appeared on the show in November that same year, but Lorne informed him that he was only entitled to $750. When John Lennon was assassinated on December 8, 1980, all hopes faded to mourning with the thought that we would never see the likes of The Beatles, or any other group, having the same impact again.

Books: *The Beatles Anthology* The Beatles (Chronicle Books, 2000)
Video: *The Beatles: Eight Days a Week* (Apple, 2016)

SOUTHERN ROCK

R ock 'n' Roll music started in the South with the likes of
Elvis, Chuck Berry, Bo Diddley, and many others but
the British invasion, along with Folk and Psychedelic
music, moved the focus to Liverpool, San Francisco, and other
large cities around the world. The Southern Rock that
emerged in the late '60s and early '70s was a merging of Rock,
Country, and Blues styles placing a strong emphasis on vocals
and electric guitar. Early standouts were the Allman Brothers,
Canned Heat, Black Oak Arkansas, and the Marshall Tucker

Band. As the '70s progressed, a harder version of Southern Rock emerged with Lynyrd Skynyrd, The Outlaws, and ZZ Top topping the charts. New Southern Rock continued to appear in the '80s, '90s, and beyond with the likes of Molly Hatchet, 38 Special, the Georgia Satellites, Kid Rock, and Kings of Leon.

Southern Rock peaked in the '70s, and with few exceptions, has been relegated to the Classic Rock category. That does not mean it is no longer relevant. The influence of the Southern Rock pioneers is evident in Rock/Country music today as well as the world of Heavy Metal with bands like Norma Jean and Every Time I Die. As the mantle of Southern Rock is passed from generation to generation, other influences, such as Jazz and even Classical music, create new, fresh sounds to thrill fans all over the world.

Gregg Allman   ZZ Top

Books:	*Southbound: An Illustrated History of Southern Rock* Scott B. Bomar (Backbeat Books, 2014) *Rebel Yell: An Oral History of Southern Rock* Michael Smith (Mercer University Press, 2014)
Video:	*Rockpalast: 30 Years Of Southern Rock* (SPV, 2009)

Swamp Rock

Swamp Rock is a fairly narrow, but important category in the history of Rock. Its one and only major player is Creedence Clearwater Revival who defined the genre. The band was short lived, but their first five albums formed the bedrock of a sound that, despite their San Francisco roots, oozed Blues and evokes imagery of southern bayous and voodoo incantations that still are played heavily on Classic Rock radio stations. Unfortunately the band cut a bad deal with their record company, with them losing the rights to their own songs, resulting in multiple lawsuits and bitter feelings.

Books:	*Bad Moon Rising: The Unauthorized History of Creedence Clearwater Revival* Hank Bordowitz (Chicago Review Press, 2007) *Fortunate Son: My Life, My Music* Fogerty/McDonough (Little, Brown and Company, 2015)
Listen to:	*Creedence Clearwater Revival* Creedence Clearwater Revival (Fantasy, 1968) *Bayou Country* Creedence Clearwater Revival (Fantasy, 1969) *Green River* Creedence Clearwater Revival (Fantasy, 1969) *Willy and the Poor Boys* Creedence Clearwater Revival (Fantasy, 1969) *Cosmo's Factory* Creedence Clearwater Revival (Fantasy, 1970)

FESTIVALS

S tarting in the mid-to-late '60s, open air, outdoor concerts featuring multiple bands over multiple days started to appear modeled on previous Jazz festivals. The hippie, counter-culture, and youth oriented events took on a life of their own with many historic festivals occurring in the '60s and '70s. Throughout the '60s, these events were referred to as "Pop festivals," despite the Rock 'n' Roll lineups. A separate book would be needed to do justice to significant festivals over the years, so I will focus on the most historic here.

Monterey International Pop Festival

June 16–18, 1967

Held in Monterey, California, in a relatively small venue with 8,500 people crammed in a space designed for 7,000, Monterey had many significant performances. It was the first major American appearance for The Who and Jimi Hendrix, the first large concert for Janis Joplin, and the first major appearance for Otis Redding. Generally considered to have kicked off the "summer of love," there were 33 performers including Jefferson Airplane, The Mamas and the Papas, Eric Burdon and the Animals, and the Grateful Dead.

Woodstock Music & Art Fair

August 15-18, 1969

Originally scheduled for three days, but splashing into a fourth, Woodstock is the granddaddy of all American festivals. There were larger, and maybe even better, festivals during the '60s and early '70s, but none were as well publicized, recorded, or filmed. More than 400,000 fans descended on Max Yasgur's 600-acre farm[40] for what was billed as "3 Days of Peace & Music" and, for the most part, that is what was delivered. A few days before the event, the promoters had to decide whether to finish the stage or put up fences and ticket booths first. Once tens of thousands of people started showing up early, they never got their fences up and it became a free festival. The festival was opened by Sri Swami Satchidananda with a short speech condemning the Vietnam war and

---

[40] The event had been planned for the area of Woodstock, New York, but the promoters suffered disappointment after disappointment obtaining formal permission. During the process, they kept promising no more than 50,000 attendees. Max's farm in Bethel, NY, ended up being the perfect location with the hillside forming a natural bowl shape to look down upon the stage.

reminding the audience that they were here to make the world, not break it.

Swami opening at Woodstock Music & Art Fair

Thirty-three bands played around the clock, only holding things up for some pretty nasty rain storms. The resulting quagmire of mud dampened spirits somewhat and the delay pushed Jimi Hendrix's show-closing performance into the next day after most of the crowd had departed. The remaining 30,000 fans saw a two-hour Hendrix set that is held up as the nexus of the '60's counterculture movement and is considered one of the most important events in Rock 'n' Roll history.

Altamont Speedway Free Festival

December 4, 1969

During The Rolling Stones' 1969 tour, they were accused of having high ticket prices. In response, they planned to close the tour with a free concert. Jefferson Airplane and the Grateful Dead joined in, hoping to bring some of the Woodstock magic to the west coast. Additional acts scheduled were Santana; The Flying Burrito Brothers; and Crosby, Stills, Nash & Young. After several changes in venue, the Altamont

Speedway was chosen only two days before the show. The change did not allow planning for a proper stage, sufficient portable toilets, or medical tents. The major problem with the stage was that it was only 39 inches high since it was intended to be on a rise at a previous location and there was no security gap between the stage and the audience. Due to the low stage, The Rolling Stones' management hired the Hell's Angels motorcycle gang (at the recommendation of Jefferson Airplane and the Grateful Dead) to protect the stage. Their compensation was $500 worth of beer.

During the day, as the Angels drank more and more, the situation deteriorated with many fights occurring between the Angels and the crowd. During Jefferson Airplane's set, their guitar player jumped off the stage to help stop a fight and was knocked unconscious. After hearing what happened, the Grateful Dead decided not to play and left. By the time The Rolling Stones took the stage, things had descended into chaos. One attendee was roughed up by the Angels for trying to get on stage. He left and returned with a pistol. Upon seeing him raise his hand with the gun, an Angel pulled out a knife and stabbed him multiple times. The gun was turned over to the police. Three other people died at the concert (one drowning and two hit-and-run). The whole event has gone down as one of the darkest days in Rock history.

Isle of Wight Festival

August 26-31, 1970

In the third (and final) year of the festival in the 20th century, it was a monster show on an island in the south of England with over 600,000 attendees and over 50 bands. Many Woodstock performers were on hand along with The Doors; Procol Harum; Emerson, Lake & Palmer; the Moody Blues; and Jethro Tull. It was also a very eclectic show with David Bromberg, Chicago, Miles Davis, Leonard Cohen, Bob Dylan, and Tiny Tim performing. Over 12 live albums were recorded during the festival as well as a documentary film. Unfortunately the film release was in limbo for 27 years due to financial difficulties with it finally coming out in 1997.

Video:	*Woodstock: 3 Days of Peace and Music – Director's Cut* (Warner Bros., 1994, 2009)
	Message to Love - The Isle of Wight Festival (Sony, 1997)
	The Complete Monterey Pop Festival (Criterion, 2017)

AUSSIE FEVER

The Brill Building at 1619 Broadway in New York City has served as an epicenter for musical activity since before World War II. By 1962, it contained 162 music businesses where you could buy a song (or bring your own), shop it around to various publishers, go to another office for a quick arrangement and a lead sheet at the cost of $10, make some copies at the duplication office, book an hour of studio time using your choice of studio musicians hanging around, and then cut a demo. You could then shop the demo to the publishers, record companies, and even directly to the artists themselves, all without leaving the building.

The Brill Building, and another office building across the street, served as a songwriting factory in the '50s and '60s producing 1000s of songs with the likes of Neil Sedaka, Barry Mann, and Carole King, developing what is referred to as the Brill Building Sound. Three other songwriters working in the building were Bob Feldman, Jerry Goldstein, and Richard

Gottehrer (FGG) who wrote several hits for the Angels including "My Boyfriend's Back." The factory was chugging along, doing very well, but no one had any inkling of the invasion heading toward our shores.

The British Invasion, spearheaded by The Beatles and followed by The Rolling Stones, The Who, The Kinks, and many others, upset the longstanding tradition of songwriters throwing their song over the wall for artists to record. The craze for British music and the self-contained singer/songwriter model pushed most American artists off the top of the charts. FGG's business had dropped off significantly and started reviewing songs and tunes previously rejected, looking for a hit. They came across a catchy tune and, as a lark, tried singing it themselves with a phony British accent. It sounded pretty good and they recorded the song "Love Love," releasing it under the name The Strangeloves. It received some regional airplay with the listeners thinking the band was British, but FGG thought the Strangelove's run was done.

A DJ in one of the areas where "Love Love" was played had campaigned hard for the Strangeloves to appear in a live show with Bobby "Boris" Picket, Gene Pitney, the Shangri-Las, and Chuck Berry. FGG needed the money from the gig and thought they could pull off the performance, but were worried that their phony British accents would destroy any claims they were from Britain. Wondering how to make things happen, Australia came to mind. Didn't Australian accents sound British? Besides, how many Americans could say what was, or wasn't, an Australian accent? Problem solved.

FGG fabricated a full backstory for The Strangeloves. Their names were Miles, Niles, and Giles Strange hailing from Armstrong, Australia, and they were wealthy sheep herders. On their way to their first gig, they were arrested in Delaware for driving over 100 mph. With minutes to spare, their fine was paid and they arrived at the Newport News airport. They climbed aboard a private jet, taxied over to the terminal, and got off as though they had just arrived from Australia. A crowd of fans greeted them and the mayor presented them with the key to Virginia Beach. The show went well with only six songs in their 40-minute set including an 18-minute version of "Shout." FGG knew they were on to something.

FGG recorded a few rough tracks, shopped them around, and got a record deal with Bang Records, a new subsidiary of Atlantic. The producer loved the tracks and the whole Strangeloves story. One of the tracks was based on the beat from the song Bo Diddley. As the song was fleshed out, a decision was made to base the lyrics on a pornographic book spoof called Candy and the song "I Want Candy" was born, going all the way to Number 11 on the U.S. charts. The group's backstory was refined to them being wealthy but eccentric sheep herders that made millions on a cross-breed called "Gottehrer Sheep." In order to explain their total lack of similar features, the story shared that while they had a common mother, they had three different fathers.

To really put things over the top, the band dressed in black leather pants, black turtleneck shirts, and zebra skin vests. For their stage props they included boomerangs, spears, and a huge collection of African drums. Despite the curious clash of cultures, it all went over well with the fans as the group toured with the Seekers, the Searchers, Freddie and the Dreamers, and the Dave Clark Five.

During the tour, they added a reworked version of the Vibrations song "My Girl Sloopy." The Dave Clark Band liked the Strangeloves' version and planned to record upon their return to England. Feeling they could not release another song so quickly after "I Want Candy," the decision was made to give the song, now called "Hang on Sloopy," to an adolescent band called the McCoys with guitar player Rick Zehringer (later changed to Rick Derringer) giving them a Number One hit. FGG used the McCoys as their opening act and, over time, the McCoys' star rose as the Strangeloves' began to set.

Feldman, Goldstein, and Gottehrer as The Strangeloves

There is no video record of a live Strangeloves performance outside of their lip-synced appearances on some TV shows, but there are many accounts of their exciting solos on their African drums to close the show. There are also many wonderful tour stories such as Niles, the self-professed boomerang expert, displaying his skills for a Pittsburgh TV station, which resulted in a cameraman receiving 22 stitches. There also was a narrow escape from a lynching in Alabama. As the Strangeloves faded, FGG continued to manage the McCoys and write songs for others. This chapter, with its Brill Building roots and fans buying into borderline silliness, is one of my favorite footnotes in Rock 'n' Roll history.

WOMEN IN ROCK

Being in a Rock 'n' Roll band is a peer bonding experience and our society decided a long time ago that this would be primarily a male activity. As the 1960s progressed, women were allowed to sing, but rarely played an instrument. By the early to mid-'70s, there were finally some female-led Rock bands and it is important to understand and appreciate what they contributed to the Rock landscape. My criteria of straight-ahead Rock 'n' Roll for this concise list omits many great artists, such as Carole King and Linda Ronstadt, but my hope is that this list inspires you to dig deeper and discover the rich body of work from female Rock artists through the years.

Grace Slick

Grace Slick joined Jefferson Airplane, bringing a powerful, classically trained voice. There were a few other Rock female lead singers at the time, but none with the power and attitude of Grace. This, and her ability to write songs like "White Rabbit,"[41] put her in the vanguard for lead women singers in Rock 'n' Roll. Grace was beautiful, fashionable, but talked like a truck driver and was also the vanguard for substance abuse. In the early '90s, Grace left the business stating, "All rock-and-rollers over the age of 50 look stupid and should retire."

Jefferson Airplane

Grace Slick

Janis Joplin

Janis is one of the more tragic figures in Rock 'n' Roll. When she joined Big Brother & The Holding Company in 1966, she had already dealt with some severe emotional and drug issues.

---

[41] Search the internet for video file that isolates the voice track for the song and you will hear her powerful voice.

Her bluesy, rough voice was an original and made her a standout at the Monterey Pop Festival in 1967. She recorded two albums with Big Brother before leaving and recording two solo albums. She performed at Woodstock and on several other large tours, but Janis never was able to overcome her internal demons. She died from a heroin overdose, compounded by alcohol, 16 days after Jimi Hendrix's death on October 4, 1970. Her second solo album, *Pearl*, was released posthumously. Janis's influence is still felt today where songs like "Summertime" and "Piece of My Heart" continue to show future generations how it is done.

Janis Joplin

Suzi Quatro

Suzi was the first performer to hit the Rock 'n' Roll mainstream as a solo singer/songwriter. Her largest success was in Europe and England, but became well known in the

U.S. with a recurring role as "Leather Tuscadero" on TV's *Happy Days*. Seeing her open for Alice Cooper in 1975, I was thrilled by her stage presence and her straight-ahead Rock 'n' Roll songs such as "48 Crash" and "Devil Gate Drive." Suzi leaped through the glass ceiling and in 2011 said, "For everybody that came afterward, it was a little bit easier, which is good. I'm proud of that."

Patti Smith

First and foremost, Patti Smith is a poet. Her poems alone make her worthy of note, but when you add in her ability to jump between complex, intricate songs and what can only be classified as pure Punk, makes her extra special. Her first album, *Horses*, remains one of the premier Rock 'n' Roll albums. The list of musicians, male and female, that she inspired is a long one and will only continue to grow.

Suzi Quatro   Patti Smith

Stevie Nicks and Christine McVie

It would have been easy to omit Christine McVie while talking about Fleetwood Mac. Stevie Nicks was the performer who was front and center to the audience, but the pair in the group showed the various ways women could stand out in Rock 'n' Roll. Stevie is always dressed in flowing dresses (giving her performances a mystical quality) and her husky, but strong voice was very commanding. Christine has a beautiful alto voice and is an accomplished piano player. All of these attributes wouldn't mean much without songs to sing and these two ladies' song output is astounding. As songwriters, I count well over 70 songs between them and this does not include their many co-writing accomplishments. Stevie's "Landslide" and Christine's "Songbird" are two songs that always draw me in, no matter how many times I have heard them. Two ladies with very different styles whose careers merged and diverted many times over the years and have always left their fans wanting more.

Stevie Nicks   Christine McVie

Joan Jett

Joan was one of the founding members of the Runaways, an all-girl Hard Rock band formed in 1976. She initially played rhythm guitar and sang backup vocals, but when the existing lead singer left the group, she took over. After the group fell apart at the end of the '70s, Joan received some advance money for an album and used it to put together the Blackhearts group. The 1981 breakout album, *I Love Rock 'n' Roll*, and their live performances established them as a kick-ass band that remains to this day.

Lita Ford

Lita was also a founding member of The Runaways, which disbanded when Jett wanted to go in a more Punk Rock direction while Ford wanted to stay the Hard Rock course. Inspired by Deep Purple's Richie Blackmore, she started playing guitar at 11 years old and schooled a lot of men on Rock 'n' Roll guitar playing. *Rolling Stone* magazine referred to her as "'the one-and-only guitar-playing rocker chick who could shred" and songs like "Kiss Me Deadly" prove it.

Joan Jett

Lita Ford

Ann and Nancy Wilson

Ann and Nancy front the band Heart. They both sing, play multiple instruments, and can point to four decades of success. Their mix of Folk, Progressive, and Hard Rock, sometimes on the same album, truly has something for everybody. They always put their all into every show with Ann's powerful voice and Nancy's guitar being the perfect complement to each other. Their first major hit, "Barracuda," is the perfect example of this. Their influence, worldwide, cannot be understated.

Ann and Nancy Wilson

Pat Benatar

Pat's rise to fame was meteoric in the late '70s and climbed to even new heights with the success of MTV (her *You Better Run* video was the second video shown on the new channel). A mezzo-soprano capable of fifth-octave belts, her singing can hit you hard, hold you down, and make you beg for more. She greatly resented how she was objectified for the early videos and has been adamant ever since that it would never happen again. Check out "Hit Me with Your Best Shot" and "Hell is for Children" to hear Pat at her best.

Chrissie Hynde

Chrissie's rare contralto vocal range (the lowest female voice type) stamps The Pretenders' song with a unique sound. She was born in the U.S., but bounced back and forth between Europe and the U.S. for several years before putting together The Pretenders in 1979. Songs like "Brass in Pocket" and "Back on the Chain Gang" show her amazing vocal control, but she has remained averse to any type of voice instruction saying, "Distinctive voices in Rock are trained through years of many things: frustration, fear, loneliness, anger, insecurity, arrogance, narcissism, or just sheer perseverance – anything but a teacher."

Pat Benetar   Chrissie Hynde

Debbie Harry

Debbie was already a success in Europe before joining the group Blondie and riding the Punk/New Wave phenomenon of the late '70s. A regular at the CBGBs and Bottom End clubs in New York, she brought a punkish sort of class to the performances. Sure, they sold out to Disco for a brief time, but they righted the ship and influenced multiple generations of artists. Listen to "One Way or Another" to hear her at the height of Blondie's New Wave sound. During the '70s, "Heart of Glass" sounded too much like pandering to the Disco crowd, but through a more mature set of ears, sounds wonderful.

Cyndi Lauper

Cyndi's first solo album, *She's So Unusual*, was appropriately titled. Cyndi has marched to the beat of a different drummer all her life and shows no signs of slowing down. Riding the first MTV success wave, her three-plus-octave range and heartfelt songs have inspired almost every female singer in Rock and Pop today. Some people have been put off by her performing antics live and in music videos, but while just having fun onstage, she takes her music very seriously and it shows through and through.

Debbie Harry   Cyndi Lauper

Books:	*She's a Rebel: The History of Women in Rock and Roll* Gillian Gaar (Seal Press, 2nd Ed., 2002)
Video:	*Punk in England: Women in Rock* (Vision Films, 2016)
	Viva Las Vegas (MGM, 1964)

MYTHS, LEGENDS, AND THE RIDICULOUS

The Rock 'n' Roll world is full of sensational stories, conspiracies, and all sorts of flummery. Here are the ones which have stood the test of time despite not being true.

Louie, Louie

On April 6, 1963, The Kingsmen went into an Oregon studio and paid $50 to record a version of Richard Berry's song

"Louie Louie."[42] It was completed in one take and deviated from the original by a few mistakes that are now considered the correct way to play it. The single was catching on when a parent wrote to Robert Kennedy, the Attorney General of the Unites States, complaining that the song had obscene lyrics. Despite the documented lyrics on file in the U.S. Copyright Office showing it was about a Jamaican sailor returning home to visit his love, the FBI launched an investigation. After four months they determined that it was "unintelligible at any speed" and that they could not declare it obscene[43].

Zappa and the Poo Legend

As the legend goes, Frank Zappa ate poop onstage. Despite the noise level this legend generated when first heard, there has never been any evidence that it actually occurred. When Frank was asked directly about the incident, he responded, "The closest I ever came to eating s%@t anywhere was at a Holiday Inn buffet in Fayetteville, N.C."

Paul is Dead

In 1969 several Beatles fans pulled together what they were sure were clues that Paul McCartney had died in an auto crash in 1966 and that he had been replaced by the winner of a look-alike contest. Sure, there are lots of vague lyrics and images that could be interpreted in many different ways, but the most significant evidence trotted out to prove their case is the cover of *Abbey Road* where Paul is the only one walking across the street without shoes. What you hear around this most of the time is: "Many cultures bury their dead without shoes." Looking at all of the photos from the cover photoshoot (three pictures taken going one way and three going the opposite way), Paul also took pictures with sandals on during the

---

[42] As per the writer of the song, Richard Berry, there should be no comma in between.

[43] Interesting side note: 54 seconds in, you can hear the drummer yell "F*#k" when he dropped his drumstick.

return trip. The picture selected for the cover was the only one that showed all four members with their legs evenly spaced.

The Lizard King is Alive!

Jim Morrison died in a Paris apartment on July 3, 1971. He had been taking a sabbatical with his girlfriend, Pamela Courson, to lose weight and refresh his mind. There were some interesting circumstances surrounding his death, such as the delay in the media knowing (six days), the lack of an autopsy (not required in France), and Pamela telling the authorities that he had no immediate family (allowing a quick burial) despite his parents being alive. Since then he has been reported in the Australian Outback, Tibet, and the American midwest (where he rides rodeo). With no real evidence to the contrary we can only assume that the Lizard King is no more.

Mama Choked on a Sandwich?

After leaving The Mamas & the Papas, Cass Elliot (a.k.a. Mama Cass) started a solo career that was on a fast track upwards. On July 29, 1974, during a two-week run at the London Palladium, a coroner was called to her hotel. Finding Cass dead in her bed and seeing a sandwich on the nightstand, he drew a conclusion that the obese Mama had choked to death on the sandwich. The only problem with this conclusion is that the sandwich was untouched (as per the police report) and that the autopsy revealed she had suffered a heart attack.

A Cow's Tongue?

Gene Simmons of KISS helped revolutionize Rock showmanship with the band's show including pyrotechnics, fire breathing, and fake blood spitting. One of Gene's most prominent physical features is a very long tongue (which plays heavily for the blood spitting). It was so long that rumor abounded in the mid-'70s that he had grafted a cow's tongue to his own. If you have ever seen a real cow's tongue you would know how silly the thought is, but the rumor still lives.

Dark Side of the Rainbow

Diehard fans maintain that Pink Floyd's *Dark Side of the Moon* cadence was built around the 1939 movie *The Wizard of Oz*. There are many suggestions on where to start the album to sync with the movie, but I recommend just after the MGM lion's third roar. Sure... some poignant moments are punctuated by a few areas of the album, but there are a lot of sections that do not synchronize. Pink Floyd's drummer, Nick Mason, was quoted as saying, "It's absolute nonsense. It has nothing to do with *The Wizard of Oz*. It was all based on *The Sound of Music*." Thanks for clearing that up, Nick.

Audio Rorschach Test

Reversing a recording (a.k.a. backmasking) has been used for aesthetic reasons as well as a method of sneaking phrases past censors. One of the most trumpeted examples is supposed satanic messages hidden in Led Zeppelin's *Stairway to Heaven*. The lyrics in question were a bit nonsensical ("If there's a bustle in your hedgerow" and "It's just a spring clean for the May queen") but when played backwards (forwards?), it's just what you would expect – slurred sounds where human ears, looking for patterns, find them, even if they are not there. If I played a recording in reverse and it sounded like a normal statement, I would conclude it was intentional. If I play a recording in reverse and it sounds garbled with some *almost* sounding like real words appear here and there, I would conclude that it was unintentional and some people have too much time on their hands.

Keith the Unsinkable

Keith Richards, guitar player for The Rolling Stones, has a well-deserved reputation as a hardcore consumer of drugs and alcohol. His looks reflect the many years of partying, with jokes abounding that in an apocalypse, the only survivors will be Keith and cockroaches. The rumor was that Keith, in a desperate attempt to get clean for a tour, had all of his blood replaced, but no, that's not a real thing.

Robert Johnson's Pact with the Devil

As the story goes, Robert Johnson was an average harmonica player, but a crummy guitar player who wished to be a great guitar player. He was instructed to take his guitar to the nearby crossroads at midnight where he met a man (the devil) who took his guitar and tuned it. After playing a few songs with it, he returned it to Robert along with the ability to play like a Blues master. Of course this ability came at the cost of Johnson's soul. To some, Johnson's tragic death at the age of 27 was just the devil getting his due. Of course this discounts the fact that Robert spent well over a year living and studying with Delta Blues legend Ike Zimmerman. Ah, the devil is in the details...

The crossroads at Clarksdale, Mississippi

TRUE STUFF

After reading all of the fantastic, untrue Rock 'n' Roll legends, it is appropriate to include some amazing stories and facts that are actually true. Enjoy!

- None of The Beatles ever learned to read music. That's right, all of the Fab Four were self-taught musicians and only played by ear. Paul McCartney tells a story where he and John Lennon rode a bus across Liverpool to have a more knowledgeable guitarist show them how to play a B7 chord.

- When Bill Haley & His Comets first released "Rock Around the Clock" in the Spring of 1954, most people had never heard of Rock 'n' Roll and the record company had a hard time describing the song. What they went with on the label: "Novelty Foxtrot."

- When he made a mistake recording "Hey Jude," Paul McCartney can be heard saying, "Oh, f...ing hell," at 2:58 into the song.

- In 1963, a fraternity at Janis Joplin's college voted her "The Ugliest Man on Campus."

- MGM canceled the contracts for 18 of their recording acts in 1970 because they believed that they promoted hard drugs in their songs. The 18 acts included Steve Lawrence and Eydie Gorme who were clean, popular singers, but kept Eric Burdon and War, who made many drug references, in their catalog.

- To promote the Marvel comic book based on their onstage characters, KISS had blood drawn backstage at the Nassau Coliseum, then flew to the Marvel plant in Buffalo and poured the vials into a red ink vat. The whole process was witnessed and documented by a notary. A rumor surfaced later that the blood-enhanced ink was accidently used for a *Sports Illustrated* run.

- AC/DC guitarist Malcolm Young worked in a bra factory as a sewing-machine mechanic. I wonder what songs that inspired...

- The Nirvana song "Smells Like Teen Spirit" was inspired by a deodorant. Teen Spirit is a sweet scented deodorant made by Mennen (later by Colgate/ Palmolive) marketed to adolescent girls. Kathleen Hanna (lead singer of the punk band Bikini Kill), spray painted "Kurt smells like Teen Spirit" on his wall. At the time the song was released, Kurt Cobain allegedly had no idea that the brand even existed; when he did find out, he was rather upset that the song had been named after a line of deodorant.

- The Rolling Stones' tongue logo was inspired by the Indian Hindu goddess, Kali The Destroyer. Lead singer Mick Jagger wanted something that depicted never-ending energy and Kali is generally represented with a large mouth with her tongue sticking out.

- Lou Reed released an album called *Berlin* in 1973, which included a song called "The Kids" about children being taken away from their mother. Reed and his producer, Bob Ezrin, included the sounds of real children crying and screaming in the song, and rumors appeared that Bob had recorded the sounds after telling his own kids that their mother had died. An alternate rumor was that he locked them in a cupboard to capture their screaming. Very real screams can be heard near the six-minute mark and while the cries are from Ezrin's kids, it was a regular bedtime temper tantrum that he recorded.

- Eric Clapton wrote the song "Layla" as a method to steal George Harrison's wife, Pattie Boyd. Now George's marriage was already on the rocks when Eric wrote his proclamation of his love for her, but Pattie decided to stay with George. Depressed by the rejection, Eric used heroin to escape for more than four years. Eric and Pattie did eventually spend eight years together as a couple, but that too ended as another casualty of Rock 'n' Roll.

- The Beatles had two concerts to play in the Philippines, but unknown to the band and staff, the concert promoter had promised Imelda Marcos that the band would attend a breakfast reception at the palace. Their manager had formally declined the request, but the next morning their doors were pounded on, demanding they go to the palace immediately. The demands were ignored much like other manic pleas on the road. They got the clue something was wrong when requests for room service were ignored. TV news programs were reporting it as a snub to the first family and after the concerts went off without any problems, it all went bad very quickly. Police protection vanished, porters refused to handle their equipment at the airport, and their road manager was roughed up. Glad to get out, the group vowed to never play there again and no member ever has.

- The first British Rock album to have lyrics to every song printed on the album was The Beatles' *Sgt. Pepper's Lonely Hearts Club Band.*

- Jimi Hendrix was the highest-paid performer at Woodstock. He was paid $18,000, followed by Blood, Sweat & Tears with $15,000. Joan Baez and Creedence Clearwater Revival received $10,000 each with the other 25 bands getting $7,500 or less. Near the bottom of the list is Santana who got $750.

- Ozzy Osbourne has many legends swirling about him. Here are some of the true ones:

  o Meeting with executives in 1981 after consummating a record deal, some doves were to be released. Being very intoxicated, he chose to instead bite off the heads of two doves, spitting them out and grinning.

  o In 1982, a live bat found its way to the stage. Thinking it was rubber, Ozzy put its head in his mouth and waved it about, eventually biting the head off. I guess the rabies shots he had to endure explain his being arrested for urinating on an Alamo monument later that year.

○ While meeting with German record executives, Ozzy stripped all his clothes off, performed a Nazi goosestep on a table, and urinated in the exec's wine carafe. Well, I'm sure it was a nice carpet so he had no choice.

▪ Charles Manson wrote a song for The Beach Boys! That's right, *the* Charles Manson was an aspiring songwriter who made an acquaintance with Dennis Wilson of The Beach Boys. Dennis bought the rights to Manson's song "Cease to Exist," reworked it into The Beach Boys' style, modified some lyrics, and released it as "Never Learn Not to Love." Manson was infuriated that the lyrics were changed, but was jailed before he could do anything about it.

▪ In order to get out of a bad record contract, Van Morrison recorded 36 songs in one day in 1967. The songs were complete gibberish. They were out of tune and included lyrics about ringworms and past due royalty payments. Lesson learned: Don't tick off the Irish troubadour.

LIVE ALBUMS

S tudio albums are the mainstay of the music business where artists can perform take after take or use studio technology to duplicate the version of a song they have in their head. In a live presentation, it is what it is, and for me, that's where the rubber meets the road on an artist's ability. I recognize that some recordings were never intended to be performed live, but these are few and far between. For me, it's not about recreating the studio version of a song during a performance. It's about creating an experience where artist and audience come together with shared moments that resonate for all participants. Live albums can help recreate some of those moments or be the catalyst for new ones. Some artists broke through to major fame based on a recorded live performance (Cheap Trick, KISS, and Peter Frampton jump to mind). Here is a starter list (in no particular order) of significant live albums. Pick a few, sit back, listen, and enjoy!

Alive! – **KISS** (Casablanca, 1975)

KISS was on the cusp of failing, financially, before their first live album pushed them into the superstar category. Sure, they dubbed some vocals and other mistakes, but the major adjustment was altering the noise of the audience to make it feel more like you were in the crowd watching the show. Truly a landmark live album.

Live at the Star Club, Hamburg – **Jerry Lee Lewis** (Philips, 1964)

Jerry's piano playing is on fire for this album and his electric performance comes through loud and clear. It's long considered one of the best Rock 'n' Roll live albums ever.

Performance Rockin' the Fillmore – **Humble Pie** (A&M, 1971)

Humble Pie was the resident fill-in band for the Fillmore with some success, but when this release captured the energy of the band, it propelled them to the next level. The closing song, "I Don't Need No Doctor," will always show up in my list of top live songs.

Live at the Full House – **J. Geils Band** (Atlantic, 1972)

A raw, bluesy performance that draws you in and holds you tight from first note to last. The instrumental "Whammer Jammer" changed my opinion of harmonica playing forever. Hearing this in my formative years was a blessing.

Frampton Comes Alive! – **Peter Frampton** (A&M, 1976)

Peter had been the lead guitarist for Humble Pie, but decided he wanted to be a solo act. The reasonably-priced release was the top album of 1976. The 14-minute version of "Do You Feel Like We Do" included the use of a talk box (a device that uses a tube allowing the player to shape the frequency content) to make it sound like his guitar was talking.

One More from the Road – **Lynyrd Skynyrd** (MCA, 1976)

With band members dying in a plane crash the following year, this is the best record we have of a white hot performance by some good ole boys who knew how to write and perform Rock 'n' Roll with a southern flavor. The live version of "Free Bird" has echoed through multiple generations and represents the pinnacle of Southern Rock.

Raunch 'N' Roll – **Black Oak Arkansas** (Atco, 1973)

While they had four guitar players who had trouble sounding like one good one, I have to include this album for a couple of reasons. First and foremost, the energy is palpable. You feel like you are working up a sweat in the middle of the audience. Second, Jim Magrum's voice/growl resonates through and through. Third, Tommy Aldridge's drum solo is among my favorites. Fourth (and most important), they were my first headlining band in concert, putting them on my forever favorite list.

On Your Feet or On Your Knees – **Blue Öyster Cult** (Columbia, 1974)

BOC had two other good, live albums, but this one from before the release of "Don't Fear the Reaper" has them at their Heavy

Metal best. The guitar workout will put this into part of a regular rotation for Rock 'n' Roll historians.

Made in Japan – **Deep Purple** (Warner Bros., 1973)

Originally intended solely for the Japanese market, it sounded so good, that the rest of the world got to hear it. Deep Purple, with its best lineup, is hard to beat.

Live Bullet – **Bob Seger** (Capitol, 1976)

After almost 15 years as a successful local Michigan act, this pushed Bob Seger into the big time. From funky versions of Van Morrison songs to "Turn the Page," a dark story of life on the road, *Live Bullet* captures an enthusiastic band in front of an appreciative audience. A must listen for everyone.

Absolutely Live – **The Doors** (Elektra, 1970)

Listening to this almost 50 years after it was recorded, Jim Morrison's charisma still amazes me. The rest of the band is great, especially Ray Manzarek playing all bass notes with one hand (a.k.a. "Lefty") while still covering his organ work and a lot of great Doors' classics are here. The main reason for listening to this album is the interlacing of music with poetry for the "Celebration of the Lizard," which took a whole side of an album when first released.

As Recorded at Madison Square Garden – **Elvis Presley** (RCA, 1972)

One of Elvis' better live albums captures the vibe of his show at his artistic and performing peak. From the introductory notes of "Also Sprach Zarathustra" (theme from *2001: A Space Odyssey*) to the closing with "Can't Help Falling in Love," you know you are listening to a special performance. Interestingly, this album came out of one performance rather than the typical practice of piecing together the best performances from several shows.

Welcome Back, My Friends, to the Show That Never Ends ~ *Ladies and Gentlemen - Emerson, Lake & Palmer* – **Emerson, Lake & Palmer** (Manticore, 1974)

After seeing Emerson, Lake & Palmer close out the 1974 California Jam festival on ABC's *In Concert* TV show, I became an instant fan. While I enjoyed their studio albums, I wore out the vinyl on this triple-album live set several times. Yes, it's a bit self-indulgent at times, but the rest of it makes it worth the trip. High points: Greg Lake's acoustic versions of "Still, You Turn Me On" and "Lucky Man," along with "Karn Evil 9" (1st, 2nd, and 3rd Impressions). The mix is a bit off and you feel like you are listening up high in the back of the arena, but if you enjoy any of ELP's music, you will enjoy this set.

Just One Night – **Eric Clapton** (RSO, 1980)

Eric has put out many great live albums over his stellar career, but it is *Just One Night* that captures the intensity of his guitar playing and the electricity he puts behind his performances. Long live Slowhand!

Running On Empty – **Jackson Browne** (Asylum, 1977)

With a theme of the album being life on the road, Jackson Browne not only recorded tracks on stage. He also recorded tracks backstage, on the tour bus, and in hotel rooms. Many diehard JB fans don't care for the album since they feel it does not show him at his best. I have to disagree and state that it is Jackson at his most glorious. Give it the attention it deserves.

How The West Was Won – **Led Zeppelin** (Atlantic, 2003)

Recorded from two dates on their 1972 tour, this album captured the band at their artistic peak. There have been tons of bootlegs and other less-inspired live albums from Zep, but none bring it all home like *How the West Was Won*. This album set allows you to time travel back to July of 1972 to hear them on tour for the *Led Zeppelin IV* album. All the songs and riffs we know so well, played with a live edge confirm Zep's role as one of the best Rock bands ever.

The Delicate Sound Of Thunder – **Pink Floyd** (Columbia, 1988)

Most Floyd fans will look to 1995's *Pulse* album for live versions of their favorites, but I believe *The Delicate Sound of Thunder* to be much better. *Pulse* has slightly better sound quality, but *Thunder* has a smoother feel to it and the best live version of "Comfortably Numb." Another distinction is *Thunder* became the first Rock album to be played in space. It was the only official Floyd release in the Soviet Union and the cosmonauts took it aboard Soyuz TM-7.

Live Killers – **Queen** (EMI, 1979)

Queen's first live album has songs from all previous seven albums and some special songs, such as a 12-minute version of "Brighton Rock," showcasing Brian May's guitar work. This is yet another early live album where the quality does not compare with later recordings, but for me, captures the feeling of an early, classic Queen show.

Double Live Gonzo – **Ted Nugent** (Epic, 1978)

The Motor City Madman's first live album gives you a feel for the high-energy show he put on in the '70s. Things kick off fast and furious, never letting up. Having seen Ted several times throughout the '70s, this album is my go-to Nugent fix.

The Live Anthology – Tom Petty & the Heartbreakers (Reprise, 2009)

Culled from three decades of recordings, *The Live Anthology* serves as the record of truth as to Tom and the band's ability to take their audience on a wild ride and show how tight they have played over the years. It is fun to hear how they ignored the '80's musical fads and continued to bring straightforward Rock 'n' Roll. With this album set, Tom Petty & the Heartbreakers represent the best Rock 'n' Roll has to offer.

Fandango – ZZ Top (London, 1975)

While only half of *Fandango* is live (with the other half being some of ZZ's best studio work), the live half makes it worth all Rock 'n' Roll fans' time to give it a listen. Guitarist Billy Gibbons delivers ragged Blues riffs that could cut concrete and the other band members provide the bluesy backbone that had me playing this, almost non-stop, during the summer of '75.

Cheap Trick at Budokan – *Cheap Trick* (Epic, 1979)

Initially planned as a Japanese-only release, "Cheap Trick at Budokan" had 30,000+ imports to the U.S., triggering the release of the band's largest commercial success. Their combination of Punk, Pop, and power chords are a very satisfying mix.

MTV Unplugged in New York – Nirvana (Sony, 1994)

As the '80s wound down, MTV looked to stir things up a bit with a show where Rock bands would play acoustic sets of their hits. Almost all of the shows were forgettable with the exception of Nirvana's. They went against the show's formula in a few ways. First, Kurt Cobain insisted that his guitar be run through his Fender amp and effects pedal. Second, the set list was comprised of lesser-known songs including six covers. Third, unlike other artists appearing on the show, Nirvana filmed the show in one take. Cobain was suffering from drug withdrawal at the time, giving his performance an extra edge. The closing song, "Where Did You Sleep Last Night," has grit and pain that is palpable.

AFTERWORD

Writing this book has been both a joy and torture to me. The joy came from reliving wonderful, musical memories from my life and learning more about them. The torture came from having to choose what to keep and what to omit. I always had to remind myself that this was supposed to be a *concise* history of Rock 'n' Roll. Hopefully you have enjoyed at least portions of the book and learned something you did not know before. A couple of points I would like to make:

1. Recognize that you have a 50-year library of Rock 'n' Roll to discover. There will be gems and there will be clinkers, but finding the gems make it all worthwhile.

2. Listen to other's recommendations and be free with your own. This cross-pollination of tastes is good for everyone.

3. Be open to music genres you normally would not listen to. You never know when you may be stepping over a gem.

4. Teach your kids and their kids about the history of music. It's a magical moment when the love for a piece of music spans generations.

I have tried to give you paths for learning more about Rock 'n' Roll, but my number one recommendation is to visit the Rock 'n' Roll Hall of Fame in Cleveland, Ohio. Their rotating displays and special exhibits always keep things fresh and they have some wonderful educational programs for kids.

If you want to jumpstart your Rock 'n' Roll education, the best suggestion I have to offer is watching *The History of Rock 'n' Roll* DVD set from Time-Life. It's 10 hours of well-done clips, stories, and interviews. It only takes you up to 1995, but even if you only enjoyed small portions of this book, you will love this set.

So you might be asking yourself what current groups a person obsessed with Rock 'n' Roll history listens to. Good question – I'm glad you asked. I would first have you ask yourself this question: what new music today do you think will be embraced by listeners 30-40 years from now? I am confident that some of today's music will be a part of other generations' soundtracks, but I do not think it will be in the same way that the '60s and '70s breakout music has been for current generations. At the time, when one wonderful album appeared after another, we just thought that's the way it is and the way it would always be.

While Geezer Rock continues to thrive, I am drawn to current bands such as the Foo Fighters. They know how to write a great melody with a good hook and still include an edge that the Hard Rock side of me loves. In my eyes, Dave Grohl has proven to be the 21st century's first major, renaissance man in music. His music spans several different genres and he is constantly willing to change things up and try something different. It's not always a home run, but it's always interesting and worth a listen. He has also worked to document Rock history with videos such as *Sound City* and his *Sonic Highways* HBO series. Another band that draws me in, album after album, is Seether. Their ability to write beautiful songs in a Hard Rock vein, I believe, will stand the test of time.

OK, well that's it. I gave it my best shot to provide a concise history of Rock 'n' Roll. Now it's all on you. You can be content with what you learned and be able to discuss Rock history with others... *or* you can use this as a jumping off point to broaden your horizons further: Take the road trips, read the books, watch the documentaries, and most important of all, listen to the music, new and old. Music feeds the soul and gives us a vehicle to connect with others. Don't waste it.

Want to share your passion about Rock 'n' Roll? Want to complain/laud what you've read? Want to let me know what I screwed up? Want to share your Rock 'n' Roll story? Hit me at Kevin@kwbuck.com – I look forward to hearing from you.

Cheers!!

INDEX

IMAGE CREDITS

For images requiring attribution, the following license types were used (visit URL below to view license detail):

Creative Commons Attribution-Share Alike 2.0 Generic (CC BY-SA 2.0)
https://creativecommons.org/licenses/by-sa/2.0/deed.en

Creative Commons Attribution-Share Alike 3.0 Unported (CC BY-SA 3.0)
https://creativecommons.org/licenses/by-sa/3.0/deed.en

Creative Commons Attribution-Share Alike 4.0 International (CC BY 4.0)
https://creativecommons.org/licenses/by/4.0/deed.en

GNU Free Documentation License, version 1.2 (GFDL)
https://commons.wikimedia.org/wiki/Commons:GNU_Free_
Documentation_License,_version_1.2

Cover Images:

"Avenged Sevenfold" by Dulguun7 is licensed under CC BY-SA 4.0
https://commons.wikimedia.org/w/index.php?curid=47107492

"Billy Gibbons" by Alberto Cabello is licensed under CC BY 2.0
https://commons.wikimedia.org/w/index.php?curid=41830209

"Feurengel" by Feuerhexe is licensed under GFDL
https://commons.wikimedia.org/w/index.php?curid=61830272

"Foo Fighters" by Danazar is licensed under CC BY-SA 3.0
https://commons.wikimedia.org/w/index.php?curid=45589592

"Lenny Kravitz" by Punx is licensed under CC BY-SA 4.0
https://commons.wikimedia.org/w/index.php?curid=37163334

"Robert Plant" by Dina Regine is licensed under CC BY-SA 2.0
https://commons.wikimedia.org/w/index.php?curid=8022602

"Jimmy Page" by Dina Regine is licensed under CC BY-SA 2.0
https://commons.wikimedia.org/w/index.php?curid=8005350

"AngusYoung" by Weatherman90 is licensed under CC BY-SA 3.0
https://commons.wikimedia.org/w/index.php?curid=6325211

Interior Images:

Page 3: "Portrait of Leadbelly," National Press Club, Washington, D.C., between 1938 and 1948. William P. Gottlieb, photographer. Public domain. https://commons.wikimedia.org/wiki/File:(Portrait_of_Leadbelly,_Nation al_Press_Club,_Washington,_D.C.,_between_1938_and_1948)_(LOC)_(5 395251967).jpg

Page 3: "Terryplane Blues" by Robert Johnson, Vocalion Records. Public domain

Page 4: "Portrait of Louis Jordan," Paramount Theater(?), New York, N.Y., ca. July 1946. This image is available from the United States Library of Congress's Music Division under the digital ID gottlieb.04721 https://commons.wikimedia.org/wiki/File:Louis_Jordan,_New_York,_N. Y.,_ca._July_1946_(William_P._Gottlieb_04721).jpg

Page 4: "The Huckle-Buck" by Paul Williams and His Hucklebuckers, Savoy Records. Public domain

Page 6: "Jimmie Rodgers" by Unknown. Public domain https://commons.wikimedia.org/wiki/File:Jimmie_Rodgers.jpg

Page 6: "Hank Williams" publicity photo for WSM, 1951. Public domain https://commons.wikimedia.org/wiki/File:HankWilliams1951concert.jpg

Page 8: "Edison Wax Cylinder litho" by Wellcome Library is licensed under CC BY 4.0   https://commons.wikimedia.org/wiki/File:Acoustics;_an_Edison_ wax_cylinder_recorder._Wood_engraving._Wellcome_V0025354.jpg

Page 9: "Andy Russell LP Favoritos," Capitol Records, 1943. Public domain https://upload.wikimedia.org/wikipedia/commons/d/d4/Andy_Russell_L P_Favoritos_by_Capitol_Records%2C_1943.JPG

Page 9: "Zenith_cube_radio" by Gregory F. Maxwell is licensed under GFDL https://commons.wikimedia.org/wiki/File:Zenith_cube_radio.jpg

Page 10: "Vintage_Regency_TR-1_Transistor_Radio" by Joe Haupt is licensed under CC BY-SA 2.0 https://commons.wikimedia.org/wiki/File:Vintage_ Regency_TR-1_Transistor_Radio,_The_First_Commercially_ Manufactured_Transistor_Radio_In_The_World_(22490767867).jpg

Page 10: "Diner Table Jukebox" by author

Page 10: "Wurlitzer 1100 jukebox," designed by Paul Fuller, 1948, metal, glass, wood, plastic. Exhibited in the Museum für Angewandte Kunst Köln,

Cologne, Germany. Public domain https://commons.wikimedia.org/wiki/ File:Wurlitzer_1100_jukebox,_designed_by_Paul_Fuller,_1948,_metal,_g lass,_wood,_plastic_-Museum_f%C3%BCr_Angewandte_Kunst_ K%C3%B6ln_-_Cologne,_Germany_-_DSC09472.jpg
Page 11: "Beach Boys' 8-Track Tape" by author

Page 11: "Cassette" by author

Page 11: "CD" by author

Page 17: "Bill Haley and his Comets" Universal International film *Roundup Of Rhythm*, 1954. Unknown. This image was provided with the friendly permission by Mr. Klau Klettner from Hydra Records. https://commons.wikimedia.org/wiki/File:BillHaley.JPG

Page 17: "The Five Satins" *All the Best*, album cover. Public domain

Page 18: "Fabian and Ed Sullivan" CBS Television. Public domain https://commons.wikimedia.org/wiki/File:Ed_Sullivan_Fabian_The_Ed_ Sullivan_Show_1959.jpg

Page 18: "Frankie Avalon" publicity photo for film *Beach Party*, 1963. Public domain   https://commons.wikimedia.org/wiki/File:Frankie_Avalon_- _publicity.JPG

Page 18: "Ricky Nelson" publicity photo, 1966. Public domain

Page 19: "Carl Perkins, Roy Orbison, Johnny Cash and Jerry Lee Lewis" from Johnny Cash Christmas Special television program, CBS Television, 1977. Public   domain   https://commons.wikimedia.org/wiki/File:Carl_Perkins_ Roy_Orbison_Johnny_Cash_Jerry_Lee_Lewis_1977.jpg

Page 22: "Elvis Presley" first national appearance on CBS Television on January 28, 1956. Public domain https://commons.wikimedia.org/wiki/File:Elvis_ Presley_first_national_television_appearance_1956.jpg

Page 22: "Bo-Diddley" by Masao Nakagami is licensed under CC BY-SA 2.0 https://commons.wikimedia.org/wiki/File:Bo-Diddley.jpg

Page 22: "Chuck Berry" publicity photo, unknown. Public domain https://commons.wikimedia.org/wiki/File:Chuck_Berry_1957.jpg

Page   22:   "Buddy   Holly,   pioneer   of   rock   and   roll"   circa   1958   by masclarovodka.blogspot.com. Public domain https://commons.wikimedia.org/wiki/File:Buddy_holly.jpg

Page 26: "Alan Freed" publicity photo published by TV-Radio Mirror, September 1956. Public domain https://commons.wikimedia.org/wiki/File:Alan_Freed_disk_jockey.jpg

150

Page 28: "Moonday Coronation Ball" poster, 1952. Public domain
https://en.wikipedia.org/wiki/File:Moondog_poster.jpg

Page 31: "Joan Baez & Bob Dylan" Civil Rights March on Washington, D.C., August
28, 1963, Rowland Scherman, photographer. Public domain
https://commons.wikimedia.org/wiki/File:Joan_Baez_Bob_Dylan.jpg

Page 33: "The Beach Boys" Ed Sullivan Show, October 13, 1968. Public domain
https://commons.wikimedia.org/wiki/File:Sullivan_Beach_Boys.jpg

Page 34: "The Kingsmen" in 1966. Clockwise from lower left: Lynn Easton, J.C.
Rieck, Kerry Magness, Mike Mitchell, Dick Peterson. The photo was part of
an ad congratulating Brenda Lee on her 10th anniversary in show business.
Public domain
https://commons.wikimedia.org/wiki/File:The_Kingsmen_1966.jpg

Page 34: "Trade ad for The Standells's single 'Dirty Water'" issued in Billboard,
April 16, 1966. Public domain
https://commons.wikimedia.org/wiki/File:The_Standells.png

Page 35: "Fanclub1967Animals2" by F. van Geelen is licensed under CC BY-SA 3.0
https://commons.wikimedia.org/wiki/File:Fanclub1967Animals2.jpg

Page 35: "Fanclub_-_The_Kinks_2" by W. Veenman is licensed under CC BY-SA 3.0
https://commons.wikimedia.org/wiki/File:Fanclub_-_The_Kinks_2.png

Page 36: "Dave Clark Five" publicity photo for film Get Yourself a College Girl.
Public domain
https://commons.wikimedia.org/wiki/File:Dave_Clark_Five_1964.JPG

Page 36: "The Rolling Stones" 1966. ingen uppgift via Wikimedia Commons CC
https://commons.wikimedia.org/wiki/File:Kungliga_Tennishallen_Stones
_1966a.jpg

Page 38: "Grateful Dead" trade ad for album American Beauty, December 5, 1970.
Public domain
https://commons.wikimedia.org/wiki/File:Grateful_Dead_(1970).png

Page 38: "Pink Floyd" trade ad for album Meddle, October 30, 1971. Public domain
https://commons.wikimedia.org/wiki/File:Pink_Floyd_(1971).png

Page 40: "Robert Plant (left) and Jimmy Page (right) of Led Zeppelin" in concert
in Chicago, Illinois, 1977, Jim Summaria, photographer. Licensed under CC
BY-SA 3.0 https://commons.wikimedia.org/wiki/File:Jimmy_Page_
with_Robert_Plant_2_-_Led_Zeppelin_-_1977.jpg

Page 42: "AngusYoung" by Weatherman90 is licensed under CC BY-SA 3.0
https://commons.wikimedia.org/wiki/File:AngusYoung.JPG

Page 42: "David_Lee_Roth_-_Van_Halen" by Carl Lender is licensed under CC BY-SA 2.0 https://commons.wikimedia.org/wiki/File:David_Lee_Roth_-_Van_Halen.jpg

Page 43: "Genesis_live_1974-11-20" by Tony Morelli is licensed under CC BY-SA 2.0 https://commons.wikimedia.org/wiki/File:Genesis_live_1974-11-20.jpg

Page 45: "Black Sabbath" publicity photo, Vertigo Records, 1970. Public domain https://commons.wikimedia.org/wiki/File:Black_Sabbath_(1970).jpg

Page 46: "David Bowie" cover art for album *Young Americans*, RCA Records, 1975. Public domain https://commons.wikimedia.org/wiki/File:David_Bowie_1975.jpg

Page 48: "Ramones Toronto 1976" by Plismo is licensed under CC BY-SA 3.0 https://commons.wikimedia.org/wiki/File:Ramones_Toronto_1976.jpg

Page 49: "Elivis_Costello_1980_1" by Braunov is licensed under CC BY-SA 3.0 https://commons.wikimedia.org/wiki/File:Elivis_Costello_1980_1.jpg

Page 49: "Harrison_and_Byrne-Talking_Heads" by Michael Markos is licensed under CC BY-SA 2.0 https://commons.wikimedia.org/wiki/File:Harrison_and_Byrne-Talking_Heads.jpg

Page 53: "Michael_Jackson1_1988" by Zoran Veselinovic is licensed under CC BY-SA 2.0 https://commons.wikimedia.org/wiki/File:Michael_Jackson1_1988.jpg

Page 57: "Subterranean_pop" by Philiphw is licensed under CC BY 4.0 https://commons.wikimedia.org/wiki/File:Subterranean_pop.jpg

Page 60: "Mötley_Crüe_-_2005" by Alec MacKellaig is licensed under CC BY-SA 2.0 https://commons.wikimedia.org/wiki/File:M%C3%B6tley_Cr%C3%BCe_-_2005.jpg

Page 61: "Slayer,_The_Fields_of_Rock,_2007" by Francis is licensed under CC BY-SA 2.0 https://commons.wikimedia.org/wiki/File:Slayer,_The_Fields_of_Rock,_2007.jpg

Page 62: "CannibalCorpse" by Chris Buresh is licensed under CC BY-SA 2.0 https://commons.wikimedia.org/wiki/File:CannibalCorpse.jpg

Page 63: "Lemmy-02" by MarkMarek is licensed under CC BY-SA 3.0 https://commons.wikimedia.org/wiki/File:Lemmy-02.jpg

Page 66: "Screaming_Jay_Hawkins" by Jean-Luc Ourlin is licensed under CC BY-SA 2.0 https://commons.wikimedia.org/wiki/File:Screaming_Jay_Hawkins_(7085741).jpg

Page 66: "The_Crazy_World_of_Arthur_Brown" by Bryan Ledgard is licensed CC BY-SA 2.0 https://commons.wikimedia.org/wiki/File:The_Crazy_World_of_Arthur_Brown_(15559408036).jpg

Page 67: "Townshend_smashing_guitar" by Heinrich Klaffs is licensed under CC BY-SA 2.0 https://commons.wikimedia.org/wiki/File:Townshend_smashing_guitar.jpg

Page 67: "Keith_the_ballerina" by Jean-Luc is licensed under CC BY-SA 2.0 https://commons.wikimedia.org/wiki/File:Keith_the_ballerina.jpg

Page 69: "Alice_Cooper_on_tour_for_million_dollar_babies" by Hunter-Desportes is licensed under CC BY-SA 2.0 https://commons.wikimedia.org/wiki/File:Alice_Cooper_on_tour_for_million_dollar_babies.jpg

Page 69: Alice Cooper with snake" performing live at Wembley Arena, London, on October 28 2012 https://commons.wikimedia.org/wiki/File:Alice_Cooper_with_snake_2012-10-28.jpg

Page 71: "Gwar at Bloodstock" by SLW Promotions is licensed under CC BY-SA 2.0 https://commons.wikimedia.org/wiki/File:Gwar_at_Bloodstock_2010.jpg

Page 71: Rob Zombie performing at the With Full Force Festival, July 2014" by Grywnn is licensed under CC BY-SA 3.0 https://commons.wikimedia.org/wiki/File:Rob_Zombie_With_Full_Force_2014_11.jpg

Page 71: "Slipknot_performing_in_November_2005" by Gene Smirnov is licensed under CC BY-SA 2.0 https://commons.wikimedia.org/wiki/File:Slipknot_performing_in_November_2005.jpg

Page 73: "Elvis Presley" publicity photo for film *Jailhouse Rock*. Public domain https://upload.wikimedia.org/wikipedia/commons/3/35/Elvis_Presley_Jailhouse_Rock.jpg

Page 74: "Elvis Presley TV Radio Mirror" performing live at the Mississippi-Alabama Fairgrounds in Tupelo, Mississippi, September 26, 1956. Public domain https://commons.wikimedia.org/wiki/File:Elvis_Presley_-_TV_Radio_Mirror,_March_1957_01.jpg

Page 77: "Juliet Prowse & Elvis Presley" publicity photo for film *G.I. Blues*, 1959. Public domain https://commons.wikimedia.org/wiki/File:Juliet_Prowse-Elvis_Presley_in_G.I._Blues.jpg

Page 77: "Ursula Andress, Elvis Presley, and Elsa Cárdenas" publicity photo for film *Fun in Acapulco,* 1963. Public domain https://commons.wikimedia.org/wiki/File:Andress-Presley-Cardenas.jpg

Page 78: "Presley meets U.S. President Richard Nixon in the White House Oval Office" Ollie Atkins, chief White House photographer, December 21, 1970. Public domain https://commons.wikimedia.org/wiki/Elvis_Presley#/media/File:Elvis-nixon.jpg

Page 79: "Elvis Grave" Graceland, by author

Page 81: "Los Beatles Recortado" by Iberia Airlines is licensed under CC BY-SA 2.0 https://commons.wikimedia.org/wiki/File:Los_Beatles_(19266969775)_Recortado.jpg

Page 83: "Brian Epstein (manager Beatles) Arrives at Schiphol" Grand Gala du Disque, 1965. Photographer, Joop van Bilsen / Anefo. Licensed under CC BY 1.0 Public Domain Dedication https://commons.wikimedia.org/wiki/File:Aankomst_Brian_Epstein_(manager_Beatles)_op_Schiphol_(Grand_Gala_du_Disque_1965),_Bestandd eelnr_918-2516.jpg

Page 83: "John Lennon, Paul McCartney and George Harrison with George Martin" publicity photo, 1966. Public domain https://commons.wikimedia.org/wiki/File:Beatles_and_George_Martin_in_studio_1966.JPG

Page 84: "The Beatles arriving at John F. Kennedy International Airport, 7 February 1964" United Press International, photographer unknown. This image is available from the United States Library of Congress's Prints and Photographs division under the digital ID cph.3c11094 https://commons.wikimedia.org/wiki/File:The_Beatles_in_America.JPG

Page 86: "Svenska: The Beatles i Hötorgscity" Stockholm, October 1963. Public domain https://commons.wikimedia.org/wiki/File:The_Beatles_i_H%C3%B6torgscity_1963.jpg

Page 87: "The Beatles on stage" Teatro Adriano in Rome, June 27, 1965. Public domain https://commons.wikimedia.org/wiki/File:Beatles_1965_concerto_Roma_Adriano_interno.jpg

Page 90: "The Beatles Statue" by Loz Pycock is licensed under CC BY-SA 2.0 https://commons.wikimedia.org/wiki/File:The_Beatles_Statues.jpg

Page 94: "Greg Allman" performing with Allman Brothers Band, 1975. Public domain https://commons.wikimedia.org/wiki/File:Gregg_Allman_1975.JPG

Page 94: "ZZ Top performing live in 1976" London Records, Billboard, page 49, Dec 22, 1976. Public domain https://commons.wikimedia.org/wiki/File:ZZ_Top_(1976).png

Page 96: "Jimi Hendrix" performing at Woodstock. Licensed under CC0 Creative Commons https://pixabay.com/en/jimi-guitarist-woodstock-881410/

Page 98: "Opening ceremony at Woodstock" by Mark Goff, August 14, 1969. Public domain https://commons.wikimedia.org/wiki/File:Swami_opening.jpg

Page 105: "Strangeloves_press_shot" by Sheressesuzspen11 is licensed under CC BY-SA 3.0 https://commons.wikimedia.org/wiki/File:Strangeloves_press_shot.jpg

Page 106: "Grace_Potter_2015" by Mab198 is licensed under CC BY 4.0 https://commons.wikimedia.org/wiki/File:Grace_Potter_2015.jpeg

Page 107: "Jefferson Airplane" by RCA Records, *Billboard* page 2, June 17, 1967. Public domain https://commons.wikimedia.org/wiki/File:Jefferson_airplane_1967.jpg

Page 107: "Grace Slick" publicity photo, circa 1967. Public domain https://commons.wikimedia.org/wiki/File:Grace_Slick_ca._1967.jpg

Page 108: "Janis Joplin photo montage" performing on *Music Scene*, ABC Television, October 21, 1969. Public domain https://commons.wikimedia. org/wiki/File:Janis_Joplin_performing_montage_1969.jpg

Page 109: "Suzi_Quatro_at_AIS_Arena" by Jeanie Mackinder is licensed under CC BY-SA 2.0 https://commons.wikimedia.org/wiki/File:Suzi_Quatro _at_AIS_Arena_02.jpg

Page 109: "Patti_Smith_-_O2_Academy" by Man Alive! is licensed under CC BY-SA 2.0 https://commons.wikimedia.org/wiki/File:Patti_Smith_-_O2_Academy.jpg

Page 110: "Fleetwood_Mac_-_Stevie_Nicks_(1980)" by Dr.Jazz.ch is licensed under CC BY 4.0 https://commons.wikimedia.org/wiki/File:Fleetwood_ Mac_-_Stevie_Nicks_(1980).png

Page 110: "McVie_-_Hard_Rock_Rock" by Raph_PH is licensed under CC BY-SA 2.0 https://commons.wikimedia.org/wiki/File:Buckingham_McVie_- _Hard_Rock_Rocksino_Love_Northfield_Park_Cleveland_-_Friday_ 3rd_November_2017_BuckMcVieOhio031117-67_(26589367539).jpg

Page 111: "Joan Jett" by author

Page 111: "Lita_Ford" by Shadowgate is licensed under CC BY-SA 2.0 https://commons.wikimedia.org/wiki/File:Lita_Ford.jpg

Page 112: "Heart-07-28-07" by Fatcat125 is licensed under CC BY-SA 3.0 https://commons.wikimedia.org/wiki/File:Heart-07-28-07.jpg

Page 113: "Pat_Benatar_2007-09-07" by Heidy Escobar is licensed under CC BY-SA 2.0 https://commons.wikimedia.org/wiki/File:PAT_BENATAR_2007- 09-07.jpg

Made in the USA
Monee, IL
17 March 2020